Trials & Errors
The People vs. Brian Gordon Jack

Trials & Errors

JOHN D. MONTGOMERY

THE PEOPLE VS
BRIAN GORDON JACK

© 2001, John D. Montgomery

All rights reserved. No part of this book may be reproduced, stored in a retrieval system or transmitted in any form or by any means without written permission from Watson & Dwyer Publishing, an imprint of J. Gordon Shillingford Publishing Inc., except for brief excerpts used in critical reviews.

Cover design by Terry Gallagher/Doowah Design Inc.

We acknowledge the financial assistance of the Manitoba Arts Council and The Canada Council for the Arts for our publishing program.

Printed and bound in Canada

Canadian Cataloguing in Publication Data

Montgomery, John D., 1927–
    Trials & errors: the people vs. Brian Gordon Jack

Includes bibliographical references and index.
ISBN 1-896239-76-5

    1. Jack, Brian Gordon—Trials, litigation, etc. 2. Trials (Murder)—Manitoba—Winnipeg. 3. Criminal procedure—Manitoba. I. Title. II. Title: Trials and errors.

KE229.J33M65 2001   345.71'02523'09712743   C2001-900237-8

Acknowledgements

To the Honourable Alfred M. Monnin who reviewed my manuscript and composed the adjoining Foreword, I owe a tremendous debt of gratitude

Alfred Monnin was appointed a judge of Manitoba's Court of Queen's Bench in 1957. For 33 years he served with great distinction on the Trial Division and on the Court of Appeal, retiring as Chief Justice of Manitoba in 1990. His generosity with his time, the sharing of his wisdom and his devotion to the rule of law has never waned.

To Paul Johnson, a policeman's policeman and a staunch friend, I am grateful for his invaluable collaboration.

To David Wyn Roberts, novelist and journalist, for his enthusiastic support, I convey my sincere appreciation.

Jeannie Metcalfe prepared the manuscript from my quill-penned scrawl with her usual efficiency for which I thank her.

Many thanks to my editor, Rachel Donner, for her astute observations and constructive criticism.

My wife Jennifer was my sounding board, grammarian and constant source of inspiration.

The aforementioned have my heartfelt thanks.

J.D.M.
March, 2001

Christine Jack

Table of Contents

Foreword	9
Preface	11
Christine	13
Self-Portrait of a Loser	16
The Canary-Yellow Hearse	20
A Stranger to the Truth	24
The Bungler	29
Henry	33
A World-Class Pathological Liar	37
A House in Darkness	43
The Ste. Anne Connection	47
A Futile Search	52
Profiles of the Protagonists	55
Mr. Weber	62
A Case of Mistaken Identity	68
Crown Counsel's Closing Address	73
Damn the Prosecution	75
The Realm of Speculation	84
The Longest Day	93
The Verdict	96
Reversal	98
The O'Sullivan Concurrence	106
The Second Trial	113
The Third Trial	120
Much Ado About Nothing, The Third Appeal—Part One	125

The Third Appeal—Part Two	130
The Supreme Court—A Post-Mortem	133
Epilogue	137
Appendix	139
Endnotes	189
Index	191

Foreword

The author introduces his book as the saga of Brian Gordon Jack and says that it is the sorry tale of a colossal miscarriage of justice. That is strong language.

Up until a few years ago, John D. Montgomery was one of the leading Crown attorneys in the Ministry of Justice of Manitoba. He conducted many criminal prosecutions, and many notorious murder cases, including that of Brian Jack at the first of his three trials. He is now retired but still on call for special assignments.

The first trial, with a jury, was presided over by Chief Justice Benjamin Hewak of The Court of Queen's Bench. The jurors agreed that Brian Jack murdered his wife, Christine, just as the marriage was about to break up. A heated dispute arose during the late evening of December 17, 1988.

According to the accused, his wife got up, dressed and left the house in the family yellow Blazer. A search was made for this vehicle. It appears that the accused phoned in its location to police, who had previously been informed of her disappearance.

Many searches were made to find her but to no avail. Photos were circulated in the media. On December 23, 1988, two waitresses at a high-class restaurant in Winnipeg, who had never seen the media photos, asserted that she had been in the restaurant, ordered a meal, hardly ate any of it and had left.

No body or remains were ever found. She has not communicated with her children, family, friends or anyone. This is a tough case to prove.

The jury found Brian Jack guilty of second-degree murder.

Defence counsel appealed, raising 23 grounds of appeal, one being the extreme length of the judge's charge (some 11 hours).

Bail was denied, pending the hearing of the appeal. Jack remained in custody for 14 months, the sum total of his incarceration.

A unanimous panel of three judges ordered a new trial because of an isolated error in an otherwise acceptable charge.

Mr. Justice Wallace M. Darichuk, an experienced judge of lengthy service, presided at the second trial. The second jury acquitted the accused.

The second appeal clearly brought out the fact from the written transcript that when the jury, after hours of deliberation, requested further instructions as to the difference between second-degree murder and manslaughter, Mr. Justice Darichuk, by an unfortunate slip of the tongue, misdirected them. He used the word "without," when clearly he meant to say "with," a serious error for which the appellate court ordered a new trial, but only on the count of manslaughter. The Supreme Court of Canada confirmed that decision.

The third trial was presided over by Mr. Justice John Scollin, another able jurist of great experience in the criminal field, as prosecutor, administrator, draftsman and, at times, defence counsel. The jury returned a guilty verdict and a four-year term of imprisonment was imposed.

Both sides were unhappy. Conviction and sentence were appealed. That appeal was dismissed with a dissent. Again the matter returned to the Supreme Court, where a panel of only five judges stayed all proceedings because of the total length of the entire proceedings. There the matter rested with no penalty for the accused, who is now a free person.

Mr. Montgomery is unhappy with this odd conclusion to the saga. He is not happy with the pronouncements and opinions of some of the appellate and Supreme Court judges. It is his right to criticize. Judges at all levels of tribunals must accept criticism. That is part of the task and duty of judges.

He is also unhappy with some of our laws and rules of interpretation or misinterpretation of these laws, rules and procedures on the part of some of the appellate justices.

He does not mince his words. He expresses strong dissent, as he is entitled to. His criticism is cogent and apropos. He writes easily and well, with a great command of the language. The book makes easy reading for lawyers, jurists and the general public.

His comments about the administration of justice, its flaws, the work of its jurists and some of the incredible conclusions that are reached at times are worthy of thought and effort in order to correct some of the failures of the system and those who make it work. This book is well worth reading. Good reading!

Alfred M. Monnin

Preface

Yet another unrepentant killer walks the streets unshackled.

Brian Gordon Jack was granted by the Supreme Court of Canada unrestricted passage to go about his business with all the rights and privileges of any free man.

I accuse some unapprenticed yet arrogant members of the judiciary, particularly at the provincial and national appellate levels, of a naiveté and an ineptitude that leaves me still clinging to the ropes.

It is another black eye for the administration of criminal justice in our time.

Fortuitously, there are many wise and learned jurists who acquit themselves nobly in the performance of their duties. There are others, alas, who ought to be booted off the bench.

"Judge-bashing by those unhappy with a Court's ruling must stop," bleated the then-Chief Justice of the Supreme Court of Canada, Antonio Lamer, "or the already fragile judicial system will be weakened beyond repair."

As a lawyer, I find this statement to be irresponsible and fallacious.

As a citizen of the realm, I am incensed that such baseless piffle should escape the lips of one who had occupied the top rung of the loftiest judicial perch in the nation.

It is not "judge-bashing" that is weakening an already fragile judicial system. The simple truth is that it is the injudicious rulings and flawed judgments of some incompetent bench-warmers that are contributing to the decay of a once strong and effective regime of law and order.

A towering British jurist, Lord Denning, Master of the Robes, eschewed the notion that is still clung to by diverse black-robed zealots in this country: That they are members of a priestly caste and thus immune from criticism by the untutored layman.

I take great comfort in the humble reflections of this peerless judge of England's Court of Appeal: "Let me say at once," he wrote,

> that we will never use this jurisdiction as a means to uphold our

own dignity. That must rest on surer foundations. Nor will we use it to suppress those who speak against us. We do not fear criticism, nor do we resent it. For there is something far more important at stake. It is no less than freedom of speech itself.

It is the right of every man, in Parliament or out of it, in the press or over the broadcast, to make fair comment, even outspoken comment, on matters of public interest. Those who comment can deal faithfully with all that is done in a court of justice. They can say that we are mistaken, and our decisions are erroneous, whether they are subject to appeal or not. All we would ask is that those who criticize us will remember that, from the nature of our office, we cannot reply to their criticisms. We cannot enter into public controversy. We must rely on our own conduct itself to be its own vindication.[1]

This is the true story of a beautiful wife and devoted mother who virtually vanished from the face of the earth. It traces the circumstances surrounding her disappearance, the ceaseless but futile quest to find her body, and the duplicity of a sullen husband who stonewalled police and lied to them at every turn.

It is a critical analysis of the three trials of Brian Gordon Jack, who was originally charged with the murder of his wife, Christine, notwithstanding the fact that her body was never retrieved.

It is, as well, an indictment of a "fragile justice system," which failed Christine Jack, her children, her parents and a host of her friends.

For me, the saga of Brian Jack is the sorry tale of one colossal miscarriage of justice.

During the course of rendering this account, I have shamelessly indulged in what the Chief Justice has chosen to characterize as "judge-bashing." I have even leveled a body blow or two at Chief Justice Lamer himself.

I leave it to the reader to ponder whether the critical silent majority must rise up in revolt so that our "already fragile justice system" can be redeemed.

Life is but a day, a fragile dew-drop on its perilous way from a tree's summit
—John Keats

Christine

She will be forever remembered by those whose lives she touched. The days of mourning shall never end for the many souls whose hearts she captured.

"Christmas Memoriams" is published in my daily newspaper on December 24 every year. Among the mass of photographs of those who had joined the great majority, Christine Jack appeared, a winsome smile upon her lovely face:

> "In loving memory of our dear friend whose life was ended December 17, 1988."

My eyes hovered between her sweet countenance and the poignant yet simple words that accompanied it:

> "Friend, I will remember you,
> think of you, pray for you;
> and when another day is through,
> I'll still be friends with you.
> There will always be a sadness,
> often a silent tear,
> but always special memories
> of the days when you were here."

Ten years, I was startled to realize, had slipped by since my associate, young

Brian Kaplan, and I had sat down with family, friends, neighbours and colleagues of the deceased to prepare for the trial of her murderer.

What emerged from those discussions, above all else, was a profound appreciation of just how much Christine Anna Jack was loved and admired. Even for Kaplan and me, there was a sense of personal loss. The life of a generous, tender-hearted, compassionate human being had been needlessly and recklessly snuffed out.

"You will see," I said to the members of the jury, "throughout the testimony of Cheryl MacMillan and Donna Mae Henry and Aunt Lidijia Jankovec and Annette Clay and Fay Harden, and other dear friends, a portrait of a person whom you feel that you knew and understood and admired—an image of a wonderful, loving, caring mother, a mother who could never have abandoned her children, a parent who cannot now be with Kairsten and Adam—because she is dead."

On December 16, 1988, one day before she was robbed of her life, Christine Jack sat down and wrote a letter to her father and mother, Stephan and Veletei Reiter. They resided in Westfield, New Jersey.

While conducting a search of the Jack residence on December 24, police officers located the letter, together with a Christmas card which had not been mailed.

I have read this letter many times.

The English author Dr. Samuel Johnson said, "In a man's letters, his soul lies naked."

If, in fact, this is so, it seems to me that in the simple message to her parents, a very real nobility of mind and spirit was revealed.

Christine Jack's abiding love, faith, strength, devotion and tenacity, as well as an acknowledgment of her own weaknesses, were reflected in her words.

I do not attempt to deify her: I merely list some of her admirable qualities to which so many would subsequently attest.

Her letter was admitted into evidence for the purpose of establishing her state of mind in the days and hours preceding her disappearance.

I cite it in confirmation of her goodness, and for another objective, as well. It tells of a marriage in decay and a household in chaos. It is the affirmation of a fighter who was determined to overcome all obstacles in order to find happiness for herself and for her children.

Christine

December 16, 1988

Dear Mom and Dad:
I hope this letter reaches you in time for Christmas. With everything that is happening in my life right now, it seems like I'm living from one day to the next. Sometimes, even when I have plans to do something, I just can't quite manage to get it done. I'm sorry to have to put you through all of this. I really never thought it would happen to me. Please don't worry too much about me and about Adam and Kairsten, just keep on loving us and saying a little prayer for us.

I'm finding out that I have more strength and determination than I realized. I knew my decision to leave Brian is the best for me and I think, in the long run, it will be better for the children to live in a more peaceful and happy environment. My friends and colleagues at work have been very supportive. Those who have known me for a long time have also wondered how I have gone on doing everything for so long.

Do you remember Marta, our neighbour on Balfour Avenue? She came by my office yesterday to see me. She said she had been thinking about me and decided to drop by. She also felt that I had done everything and she always thought it was so unfair of Brian. Of course it's never just one-sided and I have faults, too. I never was one to fight or yell or complain. I used to do more of that but it never got me anywhere with Brian, so I just gave up. I'm not sure that I even loved him enough to try. I know I'm still angry about all the things he did or didn't do, and I guess I just haven't been able to forgive him.

I went to see a lawyer on Wednesday. She deals with family law, separation and divorce. She was excellent and maybe things are better for me than I thought. But I'll talk to you about everything on the phone. My next step is to get Brian to move out, hopefully in January. He said he can't move out until we sell the house, because he needs money. However, according to Jan, the lawyer, I don't have to sell the house and he will have to leave, either of his own free will or by court order. I would rather he leave on his own, but I'm not sure that he will. The next few weeks will still be tough.

Enough of that. I love you both so much and it meant everything to me that you understood and weren't angry with me.

I hope that you know that I will be okay and Adam and Kairsten, too.
Please have a really nice Christmas.

With love,
Christine XOXO

Any fool can tell the truth, but it requires a man of some sense to know how to lie well.

—Samuel Butler

Self-Portrait of a Loser

"It was the older one, Sergeant Paulishyn I think he said his name was. Anyway, he was the one with the pudgy face. He told me that he was the Missing Persons Coordinator. Only later did I realize that he had been bullshitting me and that he and the younger one, Schinkel, I believe, were not from Missing Persons. They were from the robbery/homicide squad.

Paulishyn explained to me that due to some procedural flaws in the investigation, he would require a full and formal statement. I got pissed off and said that I had already told at least ten other police officers everything I knew. This, he insisted, was precisely the reason for the statement, so as to avoid any more interviews regarding the events leading up to Christine's disappearance. So I agreed to give him a statement.

First of all, he recorded the date on the top right-hand corner of the page, 6:05 p.m., Thursday, December 22, 1988.

He wanted some background on myself, Christine and our kids at the outset. So, this is what I told them:

'My name is Brian Gordon Jack and I am 41 years old. I was born in Ottawa, Ontario on the May 23, 1947. I was raised there and that's where I took my early schooling. My father was an Ontario Provincial Police officer. He is retired now.

'I received an athletic scholarship to attend Lenoir Rhyne College in Hickory, North Carolina, a small city in the Blue Ridge foothills. There I graduated with a Bachelor of Arts Degree in Economics and Physical Education.

'While I was at college, I met Nancy Sporer. We were married in 1969.

After graduation we took up residence in Canada.

'I played pro football, signing first with the Ottawa Rough Riders. Then I got bounced around to Montreal with Johnny Rogers in '73 before moving on to Winnipeg. I was with the Blue Bombers in '74 and '75.

'Nancy and I were divorced in 1977. We had two children, a boy and a girl. They are both living with their mother and I am supporting them.

'In 1978, I met Christine Anna Reiter. We were married on August 23, 1980. We have two children, a son Adam and a daughter Kairsten. Adam was born on January 29, 1982. He is six and a half years old. Kairsten is four and a half years old. I'm not really sure of her date of birth.

'We've been living at our current address, 170 Alburg Drive, for nearly three years. Prior to this, we lived on Balfour, just off Osborne.

'For the past eleven years I had been running the Pro Shops in conjunction with the Fit Stops. I had four shops in five different Fit Stop locations in the city.

'When the Fit Stops went under, I was locked out. I had to do something with the inventory so I opened Brian's Racquet and Sports Wear on St. Anne's Road. It just didn't pan out. The retail end of it just wasn't enough of a challenge for me. It was too competitive, so I had to take a risk and go into it big or get out. I decided it was time to drop the fitness and sporting goods and get on with my life. I closed the shop at the end of October 1988.

'Basically, since that time, I've been unemployed and have been looking for new employment. I've been liquidating my stock and I was also doing some substitute teaching in the St. Boniface School Division.

'I have applied all over the place, but as yet I don't have any permanent employment.

'When the Fit Stop folded, all my stock was seized. I lost my income. It was tough.

'Christine was working as a speech therapist with the Seven Oaks School Division and was supporting us. I didn't think that this was placing any undue stress on our marriage up until about two weeks ago. She also had her own line of kids' clothing. She was under a lot of stress.

'Two weeks ago she was acting kind of strange—peculiar. She and Cheryl MacMillan were going to Grand Forks, North Dakota, for the weekend to get a break. When she came back, she said she didn't know how she felt about me. She had this blank stare on her face all the time and I couldn't get any answers. She said she didn't have any feelings for me and didn't want to make love any more. Boom. She didn't want to be intimate at all.

"We decided to go and see Dr. James McPhee, a therapist.

'We just sat and talked about our childhoods. Christine was very troubled and broke down a couple of times. I even found out things about myself I didn't know.

'We saw Dr. McPhee twice together. Christine, seemed frightened of me. She was just shaking. This all came on suddenly, after the trip to Grand Forks. Apparently she didn't eat while she was down there.

'There have never been any marital problems before, problems that we couldn't work out, or major ones anyway. We played squash together and did things with the children. Ever since she started the kids' clothing business, things have changed.

'I was shocked when all this came out. Cheryl told me that it had been coming for a long time because I hadn't been helping with the kids or doing anything around the house. I was always busy with the business.

'At our second meeting with Dr. McPhee, it was decided that I should give Christine some room to work things out. I remember that this meeting was just a week ago, on Thursday, December 15. We came home just drained. We had some tea and went to bed.

'On Saturday, December 17, we got some movies for the kids. That night, after they went to bed, Christine said she wanted to talk about our living arrangements. This would have been a little after nine o'clock. We sat in the family room. She told me that she wanted me to find another place to live because there was too much pressure living with me in the same house. She started to cry. She said she couldn't stand me being around her. She was sobbing.

'I told her I didn't have anywhere to go and I didn't have any money.

'I tried to comfort her, as she was sobbing uncontrollably. I went to put my arm around her, and she jumped off the couch and backed away. I didn't push it. She started to leave the room. I asked her where she was going. She didn't say anything. Then she put her coat on.

'There was no yelling or anything. Chris was never one to yell; you can ask anyone.

'She went to the garage and opened the door. I followed her to the door but she wouldn't even look at me.

'She started the Blazer. She had her own set of keys, as she drove it all the time. I have the other set of keys for the Blazer.

'I asked her where she was going. She knew that Adam wasn't feeling well. She didn't reply.

'I last saw her driving down Alburg towards Britannica. This would have been around 9:50 p.m.'

'After she left, I just sat around. I made some coffee and sat in the family room. I turned off the movie and watched the news. I pulled out the vacuum cleaner just to pass the time.

'At around 3:00 a.m. I decided to go over to our neighbours, Donna Henry. I threw on my jacket—the red one—these pants and my boots. I went over and knocked on the door. They were sleeping soundly so I just stood and looked for traffic. Maybe fifteen minutes later I went back home. My kids were just coming downstairs. They asked me where I had been and I told them, "At Donna's." We just cuddled on the couch and I put them back to bed.

'It kept getting later and later. I started cleaning and I did all the wash just to keep busy.

'I called all of her girlfriends, or as many as I could remember. Maybe she was over at one of their places or maybe one of them knew where she was.

'I called Cheryl MacMillan and Donna Mae Henry and her husband, Peter. I also called Fay Harden and Christine's Aunt Lydijia out in Selkirk.

'All these calls would have been made around 4:30 or 6:00 on Saturday morning.

'I called the police but I don't know what time it was. I was told they wouldn't do anything until she had been missing for 24 hours. But they checked and said she hadn't been involved in an accident or anything.

'I've spoken to everyone I can think of and no one seems to know where Christine is. Today I even drove through the parking lots hoping to find the Blazer. It's better to keep busy than just to sit around.

'I have no idea where she may be. It's unnatural what's happened, for her to be away.'"

There was one major discrepancy in Brian Jack's statement to the two detectives. It wasn't Christine driving down Alburg towards Britannica—dead wives don't drive.

*Death lies on her, like an untimely frost
upon the sweetest flower of all the field.*
—Shakespeare, *Romeo and Juliet*, Act IV. Scene 5

The Canary-Yellow Hearse

He killed her and panicked.

His addled brain signaled that the body had to disappear.

In his haste to load it into the Blazer's cargo hold, his shifty eyes failed to fix upon the droplets of blood dripping from the corpse and onto the tailgate.

The killer's sweaty palms gripped the steering wheel. Slipping and sliding down the snow-clogged driveway, he quickly distanced himself from the comfortable, split-level house at 170 Alburg Drive.

Cautiously, he manoeuvred his way through suburban streets, where dwellings glowed with the twinkling lights of Christmas. Once beyond the city limits, he accelerated into the darkness and onto the broad stretch of asphalt that connects the great western plain with the rocks and crevices and secret hiding places of the vast Canadian Shield.

Gripped in a headlock of fear and anxiety, he conceived his maniacal pact with the devil. The body would be swallowed up in the bowels of the earth.

Gradually, the tension eased. He had the cover of nightfall and a fast set of wheels, prerequisites for facilitating this untraceable interment.

The cemetery plot or mausoleum crypt is selected, more often than not, well in advance of the final days of the one for whom the bell tolls.

The solemn procession will wend its way at a snail's pace to the burial site. A raven-black Lincoln or gleaming Cadillac hearse will transport the departed to the church yard or memorial garden.

There was a treacherous irony about Christine Anna Jack's whirlwind deliverance to her final resting place.

The bright yellow Chevy Blazer into which her body had been dumped sped across the wind-swept flatlands while the relentless killer mulled over the disposal plan. His mission, spawned of necessity, would succeed—of this he was certain.

Suddenly and without warning, the engine overheated. The ghoulish flight would have to be detoured.

In the nick of time, the lights of Ste. Anne beckoned. A small rural community some 40 kilometers southeast of Winnipeg and a stone's throw from the Trans-Canada Highway, it nestles against the banks of the Seine River. To this day, its population hasn't risen above 1511.

The smoking vehicle sputtered along Dawson Road, the main thoroughfare through the village, and past the Ste. Anne Hotel, the exterior of which bore a striking resemblance to a Klondike saloon. It was wide open for business.

A deeply agitated Brian Gordon Jack had few options. He decided to gamble and go inside. Help, he reckoned, just might be available within.

He avoided the parking spaces in front of the hotel and in the half-empty lot on the north side. Warily, he pulled into a space 60 feet beyond.

Brenda Appleyard was working behind the bar when the tall stranger sidled up. He asked her if there was a garage or gas station open, as his truck had broken down.

"No," she told him, "everything is closed."

"I'll pay anything to get it fixed, one hundred dollars, whatever, because I have to get to Kenora [Ontario, about 200 kilometers east of Winnipeg] to pick up another truck," he said.

"What's the problem?" the cheerful bartender asked.

"Rad hose," he muttered.

Although he seemed like he was in a rush, Miss Appleyard recalled that he still wanted a beer.

"I gave him an Old Vienna," she said. "Then Roger Pilloud, the hotel owner, came over to the bar and I told him what the problem was. He suggested that I call Jim Hudrick, who has a local garage. I placed the call and Jimmy said he was on his way."

Most of the regulars who frequent the Ste. Anne Hotel pub were at their hearth sides trimming trees and wrapping presents on this particular Saturday night, for Christmas was just a week away.

While Brenda served the few tipplers who straggled in, Roger Pilloud relaxed in the lounge with Gilbert Gregoire, Patrick Simard and his wife, Murielle. Sharing a glass with friends was a rare indulgence for the affable publican, who usually bustled about attending to his patrons.

"I remember joining this guy at his table," Pilloud said, "while he was hoisting a cold one. He told me he was going to Kenora to take over a semi-tractor trailer. This guy never looked me in the eye while we talked. He was nervous, real nervous."

Patrick Joseph Simard's gaze focused on the newcomer.

"I took special notice of him because he was a stranger. He was very cold and he was asking for help. He was a white man, between 40 and 45 years old, six feet, three inches to six feet, five inches in height, heavy build, full moustache. He was dressed for cold weather. He wore a dark-coloured toque and a light-gray jacket, three-quarter length with red piping."

Sherlock Holmes would have applauded this attention to detail.

"He wore grayish-coloured pants. They appeared to be work pants. His boots were lined Bushpacs, black in colour, I think.

"Upon his arrival, he approached Brenda at the bar. As he talked with her, Roger joined them. Then, returning to our table, he told us of the stranger's problem with the radiator.

"Within 15 minutes, Jim Hudrick arrived and he and the stranger left the bar together."

There were things about the husky stranger that aroused Hudrick's curiosity and that of his young brother-in-law, Paul St. Marie, who had come along to lend a hand. Things he had said and done perplexed them.

Why, for instance, had he parked his Blazer by the Co-op when the hotel parking lot was almost empty?

Why had he insisted on driving his vehicle into the garage and then stopping it when the front wheels had scarcely cleared the door?

Why had he insisted on starting the engine and then shutting it off himself?

Why had he continued to wear the heavy insulated leather gloves in the warm garage?

"He pointed to his vehicle," Hudrick said, "which was a yellow '83 Chev Blazer with black pin striping on the bottom of each side, dark tinted windows, V-6 engine, with a trailer hitch on the back. It had rally wheels on it, I remember, because they made it look real fancy.

"When I got the Blazer up on the hoist, I went to check to see if the steering was locked. Before I could get to the driver's door, this guy shouted, 'It's fine. The steering is locked!'

"Another weird thing," Hudrick continued. "I opened the garage doors and went back to his vehicle and told him I was going to drive it into the garage. 'No,' he yelled, 'I'll drive it!' He moved it so that only the front wheels and engine compartment were in the garage. Then he popped the hood. I checked the antifreeze and saw that there was none so I filled it. I went to start it. 'No,' he loudly insisted, 'I'll start it!'

"I checked for leaks and there were none and so I had him shut the engine off. 'You must have a cracked head or leaking head gasket,' I told him. 'It may seize up.'

"He said he had to make a run to Kenora and wondered if the vehicle would make it. He was acting strange and edgy. All he could think of was getting the vehicle going. I thought he might be running drugs. 'You'll never make it to Kenora,' I warned him.

"I suggested he leave the vehicle with me and I would give him a ride to the city, or wherever he wanted to go, and fix his vehicle when I could get parts, or tow it, whatever he wanted.

'No,' he stated emphatically, 'I don't want to leave it because I have to be in Kenora tonight. I'll go a little way down the road and try it to see if it's going to heat up again, and then I'll come back and pay you, if that's okay,' he said as he backed out of the shop.

"We waited for 15 or 20 minutes and he hadn't returned. Because we hadn't been paid, we jumped in the tow truck and went after him.

"We headed east on the Trans-Canada in the direction of Kenora and, after having driven for about five miles, we saw him ahead of us. I pulled up right behind and continued to follow him. I tailgated him just a short distance, about up to the Love Nest Campground, when he pulled over to the shoulder, got out of his vehicle and rushed up to the tow truck, even before we could get out.

"He came up to the driver's door and said everything was okay because the truck wasn't heating up. Quickly, he pulled out his wallet. There seemed to be a lot of money in it. He went through it, yanked out a fifty dollar bill, thrust it at me and took off.

"We followed him east on Highway 1 for another mile or so. There was a lot of smoke coming out the back. Under the circumstances there was nothing more that we could do, so we turned around and went home."

The lanky psychopath had successfully run interference around his vehicle.

He drove off into the prairie night.

He who keeps back the truth, or withholds it from men, from motives of expediency, is either a coward, or a criminal, or both.

—Max Muller

A Stranger to the Truth

"I have known Christine since I was 15 years old," a distraught Cheryl MacMillan told police. "We are best friends. We own Kinderspirit, a children's clothing store. We are partners. Christine would confide in me over the years about most of her problems and concerns. She would also confide in Donna Henry, another friend of ours.

"I called her on Saturday, December 17 at 5:00 p.m. We were making plans for Monday night, when I was having some of our girlfriends over to my house for a Christmas party. We talked about what she would bring. She and Donna were going to make a Greek salad and a dessert. Chris was really looking forward to a relaxing evening with her friends.

The Henrys, Peter and Donna Mae, were neighbours of the Jacks. Their house was a few doors away at 190 Alburg Drive. To Donna, Christine was like a sister. She telephoned Christine around 7:40 p.m. on that fateful Saturday evening.

"Chris sounded really happy," Donna remembers. "She was just getting the kids ready for bed. There was no indication that there was anything wrong."

Her joyous anticipation of the Christmas festivities, alas, was short-lived. Within five hours of Cheryl and Donna Mae's telephone calls, Christine Jack was dead.

A post-mortem examination of the body would have revealed the primary cause of death. Without it, or a death-bed confession from the murderer, no one will ever know how she died. The place where her remains are concealed is a mystery. Its location promotes wild speculation to this day.

The smoking Blazer vanished into the darkness far beyond the village of Ste. Anne, and Brian Gordon Jack found himself alone, dreadfully alone in the middle of nowhere, alone with the bloodied body of the person he had slain—his wife, the woman he had professed to have so dearly loved.

During the ensuing few hours, he became as elusive as the Scarlet Pimpernel. Then, shortly before daybreak, he resurfaced at 170 Alburg Drive.

To me, Brian Jack is an enigma and, no doubt, shall remain so until the day I fall off the perch.

He was cast in an entirely different mould than the many killers with whom I have waltzed around the courtroom.

In my reverie, I have spoken to him many times and have said to him:

"Look, Brian, I know that there were no eyewitnesses to Christine's death save for yourself, and God of course, to whom you will have to account one day.

"I'll be very candid with you, Brian. I don't believe for one moment that you had planned to kill her. From everything I have gleaned about you, I know that she was the love of your life.

"You will remember telling that sympathetic police woman, Darlene Kashuba, that Chris said she couldn't stand living with you any more and that led to a heated argument.

"And don't forget what you said to Constable Paquette. You told him that you and Chris put the kids to bed and then went down to the family room and started discussing your marital problems. You told him that Christine said she couldn't live with you any longer, that she hated the sight of you and had trouble being in the same room with you. You found this strange because you had a great sex life up until a few days before she left.

"You lashed out at the woman who meant everything to you, didn't you, Brian? In your anger and frustration you struck her in a blinding fury. You lost it, didn't you, Brian?

"And then she fell. You saw her blood and you panicked.

"This is what happened, isn't it, Brian? And then you embarked upon that pathetic endeavour, that pitiful charade to extricate yourself from all suspicion.

"But you failed. You failed miserably, Brian.

"Don't you see that had you just telephoned the police or ambulance service for assistance, you would never have been tried for murder? Everyone would have understood that it was a terrible, tragic, accidental death.

"You are a bloody coward, Brian. You just had to protect your precious ass. So, you went ahead blindly, trying so hard to cover all the bases. Your lies, you thought, would divert the path of the investigation miles away from your doorstep."

Brian Jack's next ill-considered subterfuge was the early morning telephone campaign of deception.

The first couple to be awakened were Cheryl and David MacMillan.

"Brian called at 5 a.m. on Sunday, December 18," Cheryl reported. "I remember it was 5:00 a.m. because I woke up about two minutes before the call and looked at the clock. He asked to speak to David.

"Where is Chris? Is she over there?" Jack blurted. "She left at nine o'clock. She took the car."

David MacMillan observed that the caller sounded upset and worried.

"He said something to the effect that they had had an argument and that she had left to clear her head. He expected her back in an hour. He said he was going to call Chris's aunt in Selkirk to see if she was there."

Lidijia Jankovec, Christine's beloved adopted "Aunt Lidijia," was also roused from her slumber.

"It was about 5:10 a.m. on Sunday morning when I was awakened by the ringing of the telephone," she said. "I have both the phone and the clock by my bed and I noticed the time. It was Brian. His voice was shaking like he was crying. He said that he and Christine had had a fight the night before and that they were screaming at each other. He said she had asked him to leave and that he had said he had no place to go and wouldn't leave. They continued to scream at each other and then she grabbed her keys, her purse and her green coat and went to the car and drove off. That's what he told me."

Next in line for the early morning intrusion were the Henrys.

"The phone rang between 5:30 and 6:00 a.m. on Sunday the eighteenth," Donna Mae recounted. "Peter answered it. Brian was on the phone and wanted to know if his wife was there. I told him that she wasn't. He said that he had already spoken to Cheryl and that Chris had left the house at 10:00 p.m. on Saturday after an argument and that he was getting worried. He said he had come over to our house around 3:00 a.m. but that we hadn't answered the door."

"Then he said," Donna Mae recalled, 'I came home around ten o'clock. We had a fight and she said she wanted me out of the house. Where the hell am I going to go? I don't know where she's gone and I don't know what to do. I have already called the police.'

"He called back around 8:30 a.m. We were still in bed. He stated that Chris was still missing."

❖ ❖ ❖ ❖ ❖

Liars, like the man from Alburg Drive, pay little heed to the aphorisms of the ages. The insight of the French dramatist Pierre Corneille— "A good memory is needed once we have lied"—seems to have escaped Brian Jack.

His litany of lies continued to mount by the minute.

Fay Harden was among those whom he had called between 4:30 and 6:00 a.m. that Sunday morning, he told Sergeant Paulishyn.

"Did you receive a phone call between 4:30 a.m. and 6:00 a.m. on Sunday morning?" a detective asked Bud Harden.

"No. Fay and I were home alone and we have a phone in our bedroom," he replied. "It never rang."

During his early morning conversation with Donna Henry, Jack told her that he had already called the police. This was but another of his blatant deceptions. He wouldn't make that call for at least another 16 hours.

Departmental records confirmed the exact time of the killer's first communication with police—10:46 p.m., Sunday, December 18, 1988. Constable George Frizzell was on duty in the Missing Persons section when the call came in. Brian Jack reported that his wife of eight years, Christine Jack, had left the family home around 9:00 p.m., Saturday, December 17, and had not returned. He indicated that there had been a minor domestic dispute prior to her hasty departure. When she left the residence, she was operating the family's 1983 yellow, two-door Chevrolet Blazer, license plate 482 DGK.

Other pertinent details included her age, 33 years; her height, five feet, eight inches; her weight, 125 pounds; and the fact that she had left two children, ages six and four.

The missing person was reported to have been wearing a lime-green, long cloth coat, blue sweater, dark blue turtleneck under the sweater, blue jeans and white Reebok runners.

The officer was informed that the missing person worked for the Seven

Oaks School Division and that she had a two thousand-dollar paycheque with her when she left. It was stressed that she was terribly upset at the time she drove off.

In retrospect, Frizzell was astonished at Jack's "comparatively unshaken and relatively calm manner" while he reported the circumstances surrounding his wife's disappearance.

The cautious seldom err.

—Confucius

The Bungler

The Jackal, who claims to be the world's most successful assassin, is a professional. Before his capture, he would formulate his plan because it not only ensured the completion of his mission but his escape, unharmed, as well.

In his amateurish attempt to perpetuate the myth of the missing person, Brian Jack made some fundamental errors.

His first mistake occurred shortly after a marked police cruiser parked in his driveway on the Monday morning of December 19, at 1:09 a.m. A mere two hours had elapsed since he had alerted Constable Frizzell of Missing Persons that his wife had vanished.

Ronald Hogland and Donald Gresson, two youthful police officers in uniform, were met at the front door by the killer himself.

The Jackal, feigning near-hysteria, would have displayed anxiety, fear and yet hopeful expectation during his interrogation. The words would have cascaded from him.

"Jesus, have you found her? Is she all right? Where is she?"

Jack stood mute, awaiting comment from his visitors. When he was informed that they were seeking further information that would assist them in locating his wife, the officers were invited inside.

As the perplexed officers pulled away from the house, both expressed amazement that upon first seeing them, the husband had not come straight out and asked if they had found his wife. His nonchalance during their quest for information baffled them.

The team of Plain Clothes Constables, James Pelland and Darlene Kashuba, knocked on Brian Jack's door at 11:15 the next morning, Tuesday,

December 20—a much more respectable hour.

Their objective was to ferret out further particulars to aid the search for the missing wife.

The Pelland-Kashuba visitation unearthed nothing of significance. Jack informed them that he had been in touch with Christine's mother, Veletei Reiter, in New Jersey. He emphasized that as far as he knew, Christine did not have a boyfriend.

The essence of this interview boiled down to confirmation by the husband that his wife would never leave her children at Christmas time.

He insisted that something had happened to her.

Eighty hours had slipped by without a clue or a trace or even a hint as to the whereabouts of the missing woman.

On Thursday morning, December 22, at nine o'clock, another police officer arrived on the threshold of the Jack residence.

This time it was Detective Jay Paquette, who was admitted by the tall, tight-lipped master of distortion. Again Jack seemed underwhelmed by his wife's disappearance.

Paquette told him that this was a follow-up to determine whether anything further had come to light since the initial report. Had Jack thought of anything else which might assist the police in their investigation?

Jack repeated his story without variation until he came to the place where "she then gets into the Blazer and drives off."

He told Paquette that at that point he didn't know what to do, so he just sat around the house. He thought that "maybe she had gone for coffee or for a drive to think things out."

Then came a slight embellishment that he had neglected to relate to the other officers. He said that he made a pot of coffee and that when he was in the family room, he became so upset that he spilled the coffee on a chesterfield cushion. He continued to wait and finally fell asleep. When his wife had failed to return later that day, he finally contacted the police.

Just before the detective left, Jack stressed that his wife's disappearance was totally out of character. "She is a caring mother," he insisted. "It just isn't like her to leave the children like this."

The tenacious Paquette then drove over to Leger Crescent. He was anxious to confer with Cheryl MacMillan. Although she was not at home, he contacted her later in the morning by telephone.

She informed him that Brian Jack had dropped Adam and Kairsten off at her home around 11:30 on Monday morning, December 19. Both children had stayed with her family for the next two days, she said. Then, on Wednesday night, the father took Adam home with him, leaving Kairsten to stay with her.

During the 18 years she had known Christine Jack, she told Detective Paquette that there was no history of mental illness or drug or alcohol abuse, as far as she was aware. She was most emphatic: Christine would not have left without contacting her and she feared the worst.

Another team of detectives, Sergeant Paul Johnson and Detective Brian Cyncora, also questioned Cheryl MacMillan. She graciously assisted in a marathon question-and-answer session on that Wednesday evening, just a few hours after her interview with Detective Paquette.

Much ground was covered, both old and new.

As the officers were about to take their leave, a very distressed Cheryl MacMillan said to them: "I believe Chris is a victim of foul play. Brian told me that the car was not in good shape, that the transmission was going and that if she was stranded out on the highway, something could happen to her.

"I think she is dead. I have phoned everyone and nobody knows where she is. If she was alive, she would have contacted us to make sure her kids were okay."

There was growing speculation among some members of the Winnipeg Police Department. Things just didn't look kosher to them, and a request was made for assistance from the elite robbery/homicide squad.

A mid-afternoon meeting of the high command of the Detective Division was hurriedly convened on Thursday, December 22.

Sergeant Edward Paulishyn and Detective Loren Schinkel were conscripted. Quickly digesting the contents of the reports of the five officers who had already spoken to the agitated husband, they headed for the Jack residence.

They arrived at 6:05 p.m. The two detectives formally introduced themselves. Paulishyn, posing as the Missing Persons coordinator, had impetuously conjured up this resourceful ruse as a means of obtaining a formal statement.

Grudgingly, Jack showed them in and agreed to detail his recollection of the events leading up to his wife's disappearance.

The two officers meticulously recorded his every word.

A most revealing observation by Sergeant Paulishyn was incorporated into the body of his report. He wrote:

> It is the opinion of the writer that Jack is being less than truthful with the investigators, but he does have a knack of appearing genuine as he speaks. When talking with us, he would rarely look at us and would prefer to look around, in order to avoid eye contact.

On a couple of occasions, he went to the extreme of turning his chair to avoid eye contact.

Prior to our departing, we thanked him for his cooperation and assured him that we would do everything in our power to locate his wife.

It was casually suggested to him that we might enlist the use of a helicopter for an aerial search. His immediate comment was, "It will be all white now."

Of interest is the fact that Jack appeared taken aback at the suggestion that a helicopter might be used in the search.

It was this rejoinder above all else, however, that stuck with the two detectives. They began to smell a rat—a rat by the name of Brian Gordon Jack.

A learned fool is more foolish than an ignorant fool.
—Molière

Henry

Gloom had engulfed family, friends and neighbours. A painful foreboding had all but obliterated the joy of the Christmas season for those who knew and loved Christine Jack.

Despite the tenacity and zeal of the investigating officers, the frustrating search for the missing person and missing vehicle was well into its fifth day and still going absolutely nowhere.

The first hint of any movement came with an anonymous telephone call to the Communications Centre at Police Headquarters on Friday, December 23 at 5:17 p.m.

The phones never stopped ringing in the big city communications centres. Sharp-eared dispatchers are attuned to the voices of the frenzied, the frightened, the angry, the hysterical, the drunk and the sober. The wide-awake response is instantaneous—well, nearly always.

It was difficult to follow the informant's train of thought. His sentences were jumbled with long pauses and sighs, interspersed with numerous "ums" and "ahs."

"This was one weird call," a dispatcher later confided. "The caller was even weirder."

A recording of the taped call confirmed the accuracy of the dispatcher's diagnosis.

The gist of the disjointed message, nonetheless, was that the caller had just returned from the Salisbury House Restaurant at Fermor Avenue and St. Anne's Road. In case the police were still looking for a Blazer, he wanted to report that he had seen one in the restaurant parking lot. Although it was covered in snow, he was sure that it was yellow.

The dispatcher asked the caller for his name. After a very long pause and more ums and ahs, he finally declared that it was Henry. He refused to furnish his address.

A police car was immediately dispatched to the Salisbury House Restaurant parking lot. Paulishyn and Schinkel, who were at their desks in the Crime Division, were then notified. Schinkel and even the plump Paulishyn bounded from their chairs, snatched their parkas, piled into a squad car and gunned it toward Fermor and St. Anne's. En route, they learned that two uniformed officers had already arrived at the location and had confirmed that it was, in fact, the missing Blazer.

Parked close to the southeast corner of the restaurant, it appeared to have been there for quite some time. Snow covered the roof, engine hood and adhered to the sides. Both doors were unlocked and there were no keys in the ignition.

The rear chrome bumper and rubber moulding were encrusted with dirt, save for two rub marks exposing the shiny metal. It was the collective opinion of the attending crew that these marks were consistent with the Blazer having been recently towed by a tow truck.

Sergeant Mike Hatcher was such a nice guy that even the punks he busted spoke of him fondly.

He was on duty in the Youth Division that Friday night when Brian Jack telephoned at 9:30.

Hatcher was perplexed. Why was Jack calling the Youth Division?

"It's Brian Jack calling."

"Oh, hi there," answered the affable sergeant.

"Yup, ah, I just—ah, Cheryl MacMillan just called me," he drawled, "and said that the vehicle had been found."

"That's right," Hatcher allowed, "we found it at St. Anne's and Fermor."

Mike Hatcher lent a sympathetic ear as Jack rambled on and on.

"We'll be in touch and thanks for calling," he said before terminating the call with a friendly "and keep your chin up."

Christmas festivities were still on hold for the Paulishyn family and over at the Schinkels, too. There had been no let-up for the sergeant or his young partner during this hectic day. The candle would still be burning long after midnight.

Again and again they listened to the master tape from the communications centre and strained to grasp each syllable. Then they concentrated on the cassette tape of the telephone conversation between Sergeant Hatcher and Brian Jack.

Jack was an intelligent man, university graduate and teacher, yet he was coming across as a demented stumblebum.

"St. Anne's and Fermor?" he repeated.

"Yes," Sergeant Hatcher told him.

With a heavy sigh, Jack murmured, "at the Salisbury House where it was confirmed?"

"Where it was what?" the sergeant pressed.

"Where, where, where the—ah, the, the—some people call in." Muttering almost inaudibly, he went on. "It was—you know, I went down—I went by there a couple of times myself and never..." The sentence trailed off with a sigh.

"Did you see the Blazer there then?" Hatcher interjected.

"No, no—well, I didn't. I, I don't know." Jack babbled, "I—you know, I didn't. It didn't dawn on me but I've, I've driven all over the place back there and, I mean, uh, how could it—how could they have missed it for a week?"

The pausing, stalling, "ums" and "ahs" and the sighs on the Hatcher tape bore a remarkable similarity to the stalling technique and phraseology of the anonymous caller on the master tape.

At the onset of the investigation, a dial number recorder (D.N.R.) had been placed on the Jack telephone.

There were three or four more things that would have to be attended to before they extinguished the candle.

Checks of the D.N.R. log would have to be conducted to determine whether the anonymous call just happened to have been made from the residence at 170 Alburg Drive.

They would have to be absolutely certain that Cheryl MacMillan had said nothing to Jack about the location of the Blazer prior to her having been told of its location by police.

Two sergeants, "Big John" Speirs and "Gentleman Bob" Marshall, had already picked up the tapes from the D.N.R. and had verified that "Henry" had been at 170 Alburg Drive when his call came into the communications centre. The conveyance of this tidbit to Paulishyn and Schinkel almost made their day.

Detective Schinkel had started slugging his way through a supplementary report which somebody had inconsiderately dumped on his desk just to compound his misery. It revealed, unbeknown to himself, that Cheryl MacMillan had been re-interviewed. He yawned noisily and kept reading.

Suddenly he whooped to his partner, "Hey, Eddie. Barker asked Cheryl specifically whether she had mentioned the Blazer to Brian Jack. She was adamant. She had said absolutely nothing to him about any Blazer."

The Blazer had been loaded onto a flatbed earlier that evening and shunted off to the police garage, roped off with yellow barrier tape and left to warm up.

Just before the clock struck midnight, two exhausted cops trudged over to the garage for a final cursory view of the interior of the vehicle before the forensic experts arrived from the Identification Section to quarantine their turf.

Paulishyn opened the driver's side door and pointed to the arm rest. An old bloodhound like himself was fast to pick up the scent. There was the smear of a sticky, red substance two inches long and a half inch wide.

I don't know what you're talking about.
—Brian Gordon Jack

A World-Class Pathological Liar

He could have avoided so much misery if he had only told the truth. At least that's the way I see it. But he wouldn't. Brian Jack could compress more lies into an ordinary rap session with a pair of cops than anyone in living memory. He had elevated bullshitting to an art form.

"Brian," Sergeant Paulishyn asked, "did you make that phone call to report where the vehicle was found?"

"Huh, what?" Jack stammered.

"Brian, we have the call on tape."

"I thought all your calls were on tape."

"You reported the location of the vehicle."

"No way."

"Brian, the anonymous call came from your telephone."

"I, ah, don't know what you're talking about."

"Look, Brian, we have a dial number recorder on your telephone. We know the call came from your house."

"Oh, uh, I don't know what you're talking about. No way."

"Was anybody else at your house before you went to St. Andrews?"

"No."

"Well then, you had to have made the phone call reporting the Blazer's location."

"I don't know what you're talking about."

"Look, how much clearer can I put this to you? We can prove the phone call came from your residence. We have the D.N.R. to prove it."

"So I called it in. So what?"

❖ ❖ ❖ ❖ ❖

There is always the chance that an accused person will take the witness stand in his own defence. When this happens, one can indulge in the joy of cross-examination.

While such was extremely unlikely in the anticipated trial of Regina v. Brian Gordon Jack, I started groping to get a handle on the psyche of the prevaricator, just in case.

Volume 1 of *The Encyclopedia of Human Behavior*, housed on a bookshelf in my den, was my first reference.

"Some inept social deviants," Dr. Goldenson wrote, "seem to falsify statements so easily, so habitually and so convincingly that they have been classified as 'pathological liars.' The observer who attempts to understand this deviant behaviour is struck by the time and effort which an individual may invest in fabricating his stories and in subsequently defending his fabrication."[2]

I thought that the internationally renowned psychiatrist, Dr. Karl Menninger, might also guide me toward some understanding of the archdistortionist, Brian Gordon Jack: "There are certain circumstances and conventions in which lies and deception are permissible to avoid causing pain or unpleasant situations," he wrote. "In some games, such as poker, there is a complicated tradition about deception. The one who can best deceive other players in regard to his actual holdings is apt to be regarded as the most skillful. But the deception must be done according to certain rules. One can bluff, one can lie, one can pretend all sorts of things as long as he does not take for himself an advantage which the others have forsworn with him. One instance of 'cheating' and he is out of the game permanently. 'Play,' which reverts to undisguised aggression, is unacceptable."[3]

I could see where Dr. Menninger was coming from. Still, I didn't feel quite comfortable with the resources I had tapped, so I turned to Carlo Lorenzini's *The Adventures of Pinocchio*.

I concluded my research with the firm conviction that Brian Jack would not give evidence on his own behalf. Rather, he would slump in the prisoner's dock with a schnozzle that had grown longer than a salami.

Everyone is presumed innocent until his guilt is proven beyond a reasonable doubt. The right of a suspect to remain silent is as sacred as a sacrament, even when the blood of the victim is sticking to his fingertips.

To obtain a voluntary confession without transgressing the "rights" of an accused person, particularly in this day and age, is one tough assignment.

Whenever law enforcement officers manage to extract an inculpatory statement, even from one virtually caught in the act, they can count on being put through the wringer. They will be asked to reveal their height and weight and to recreate their body language during the interrogation. Their every word will be microscopically scrutinized by the defence for even the most miniscule hint of a breach of The Canadian Charter of Rights and Freedoms.

Few facets of police work have afforded greater opportunity for resourcefulness, intuition and innovation in getting tough guys to talk.

For nearly 40 years I have watched masters at this game. Some played it with the fervor of the evangelist beseeching the fallen to come unto the Lord, to give up a life of sin and to sign a confession. This methodology had worked admirably for the two legendary detectives in these parts, the "Reverend" Peter Vandergraaf and the "Reverend" Jack Taylor.

They got the suspect to sing in other ways too, of course: the guilt trip—and fear.

Some walk a tightrope in alluding to the benefits to be derived from "copping out."

The all-too-familiar "Mr. Nice Guy and the Heavy" combination has been overplayed both in film and on TV.

None of these gambits appealed to Sergeant Edward Paulishyn or his eager understudy, Detective Loren Schinkel.

Eddie Paulishyn was a long-time trout fisherman. Catching trout was almost as important to him as catching criminals. Perseverance was second nature to him. Persistence was his modus operandi whenever he questioned a subject:

"We were at your house the other night," he said to Brian Jack. "You knew where the vehicle was. Why didn't you tell us?"

"I didn't know where the vehicle was," Jack insisted.

"When did you find out, then, where the vehicle was?"

"Just, ah, I didn't, ah."

"Am I missing something here, Brian?" Paulishyn plodded away. "You called in and told us where it was. Didn't you just tell us that?"

"I just—ah, from Cheryl. That's it. I mean, I just sat there and said, 'It's there. It's there.' Everybody's ganging up on me," he snivelled.

"Nobody's ganging up on you. Everyone is saying, however, that it is totally out of character for Christine to leave."

"Right."

"Even you agree, Brian. If it was my wife, I'd be phoning here inquiring about her. But not you, Brian. You are the man who knows where the vehicle is. You make an anonymous phone call. Then you use a different name. Can you tell us why?"

"I was confused," Jack answered testily.

I heard tell many years ago about a rather unorthodox but effective style of cross-examination attributed to a prominent Toronto advocate. Known as "the Grasshopper Method of Isadore Levinter," it was uncomplicated. All you did was jump, unchronologically, from one subject to another in rapid succession and watch the witness become hopelessly entangled.

It's unclear if Paulishyn and Levinter ever compared notes.

"I'll be very honest with you once again, Brian," the sergeant continued. "There is blood in the back of your vehicle. We have an R.C.M.P. Crime Lab expert down examining your vehicle right now. He says it's human blood and has been there for only about a week."

"Maybe it is. I don't know," Jack sneered.

"That's what he told us, definitely human blood."

A review of the meticulous notes taken by the detective-scribe Schinkel reveals that at this juncture, the suspect contorted his face, raised his eyebrows and snapped, "You've got all the answers."

If there was one single thing about Brian Jack that troubled the two detectives more than anything else, it was his failure to ask them about his wife. Their bewilderment had long since given way to suspicion and Paulishyn made an issue of it on several occasions.

"I find something a little strange here," he said to Jack. "Whenever I talked to you and when Loren talked to you, at no time did you ever say, 'Have you heard anything about my wife?'"

"Always when I call I ask," he countered indignantly.

"Not to me you haven't," the sergeant retorted. "I called you this morning and told you we'd like to get elimination prints and the spare keys to the Blazer. My first comment would have been, 'Have you heard anything about my wife?'"

"Yeah, but I've—ah, ah, I've been doing that the whole time to everybody. The phones have been ringing constantly."

"Brian, you didn't ask me once about Chris."

"Yes, I did all the time."

During a lengthy and arduous interrogation, the old trout fisherman kept tossing Jack the same line.

> "But in all our conversations, at no time do you ask, 'Have you seen my wife?'"
> "Always, always," he insisted.
> "Look, I called you this morning and..."
> "Well, you're supposed to keep me up to date," Jack interrupted. "You know I'm not going to sit there and scream and yell at you all the time."
> "Well, okay," the sergeant said evenly, "but you had a conversation with Mike Hatcher which is taped, I might add, and you never asked about Chris then."
> "I figured the calls are all taped," Jack replied, side-stepping the question concerning his inquiries about Christine.
> "Is that why you picked up the phone several times and dialed and then hung up yesterday?"
> "I just miss hit. I just—I was under a lot of strain and stuff like that. I am, ah?" he jabbered.

It didn't take the fisherman long to hook Jack in another lie.

"When did you last drive the Blazer, Brian?"
"On Saturday morning," he said.

Mark Twain described Jo Bowers as "an experienced, industrious, ambitious and often picturesque liar."[4]

The same could hardly be said of Brian Jack. While he was, unquestionably an experienced liar, there was nothing picturesque about his falsehoods. They were unimaginative, repetitious, illogical and monotonous.

The long-suffering sergeant reverted to the grasshopper method, jumping from Blazer to helicopter.

"The comment you made that really disturbs me is when we said, 'Brian, we'll possibly be putting a helicopter up,' you replied, 'It will be all white now.'"

"Well, I didn't know what you'd be looking for," he replied unconvincingly.

Another jump:

"Brian, you're a bit of a woodsman; are you not?"
"Not really."
"Well, you have a trapper's license which you've had for a number of years."
"Well, yes, I enjoy it, ah."
"You hunt and have a bow license. I understand that you recently shot a deer?"
"Yes."
"Let me advise you, Brian, that when we found your vehicle, there was a lot of blood in it. Was there any blood in the vehicle when you last drove it?"
"I put the deer in the back. I had to."
"Why did you have to?"
"I didn't have a knife."
"Was there any blood in there when you left the truck?"
"Yeah, a little, but I tried to clean it up."
"Where did you shoot the deer?"
"Up at Bissett at the lake."
"Where is the deer now, Brian?"
"It's cut up."
"Why wouldn't you tell us about the blood in the back? Don't you think that might be an important bit of information?"
"You never asked me. I'm supposed to tell you every little detail?"

Sergeant Paulishyn asked many more questions and Brian Jack told many more lies. The old fisherman had failed to worm a confession out of the killer but, undeniably, he had reeled in a trophy-sized liar.

"It's Christmas Eve now," the weary sergeant said to his prisoner. "The cops have got you in custody. The Children's Aid Society is going to take custody of your children, and the only person who knows where Christine is, is the man who said, 'It will be all white now.'"

"Hey, you guys have a tough job!" spouted the man who had an answer for everything.

Twas the night before Christmas,
when all through the house,
Not a creature was stirring, —not even a mouse.
—Clement Clarke Moore

A House in Darkness

Ugly rumours were multiplying and dark suspicions kept gnawing at the brass in the Detective Division. Early in the morning of the fifth day of the investigation, without hide nor hair of the missing person or her vehicle, a news bulletin was prepared for the TV, radio and print media that would be released later in the day.

Four pictures accompanied the communiqué. There was one of Christine Jack as well as three shots of the van, both side and rear views and a three-quarter front profile.

The vehicle was described as a 1983 Chevrolet Blazer, model S-10, bright yellow in colour, with black pin striping running along the rocker panels between the front and rear wheel wells, Manitoba license plates 482 DGK.

The appeal was succinct:

> Winnipeg Police are requesting public assistance regarding anyone who may have observed the aforementioned vehicle being operated on the Trans-Canada Highway between Winnipeg and Falcon Lake during the late evening hours of Saturday, December 17, 1988 and the early morning hours of Sunday, December 18, 1988.

❖ ❖ ❖ ❖ ❖

The likelihood of getting an honest answer out of Brian Jack was as improbable as catching Abraham Lincoln himself in a lie, as far as Big John Speirs was concerned. He had been briefed by Paulishyn and Schinkel. Perhaps the focus should shift to the family room at 170 Alburg Drive.

"We better go get a search warrant." he said to Marshall, his equally incredulous partner.

By late afternoon, the Jacks' four-level split dwelling was literally crawling with cops. No less than six scoured the place from top to bottom, some probing about on hands and knees.

Robert Thompson and Peter Luczenczyn, two of the ace forensic bloodhounds working out of the Crime Division, scanned the family room. While they found it to be in a rather untidy state, there was no evidence, at first, to suggest that a fight had taken place there. Furniture was neither upended nor did it appear to have been damaged. But Identification men don't just gawk. They are trained to scrutinize.

Their eyes, like search lights, scanned an ornament-laden Christmas tree before fixing on a hide-a-bed standing close to the northeast wall. Suddenly, a disheveled but comfortable place designed for family entertainment had become a major crime scene.

Luczenczyn bent over the couch. Like a big red-breasted robin pulling a worm out of the dew-soaked grass, he extracted a sample of polyester stuffing with reddish staining from inside one of the seat cushions.

After stashing the stuffing in plastic, he removed a blue nylon cover from another cushion. The underside, he noted, was also stained. True to his nature as a forensic hound, he too hunted by scent. He sniffed the cover. It had a fresh, clean scent, which likely indicated a recent laundering.

Again he stooped to examine two small, dried droplets of what appeared to be blood clinging to the upper back part of an arm rest.

His roving eyes missed nothing of significance. An orange woolen blanket, neatly folded, lay on the floor in the southeast corner of the room. It too was smeared with a small amount of what this old policeman figured was nothing other than blood, and human blood at that.

He removed a minute droplet from the carpet. Then he spotted an additional globule clinging to the edge of a ceramic vase. He took a sample from this rather telling find and placed it in a plastic bag.

At this stage of the investigation, proof that what was found in the family room was blood was tentative. To prove that it was, in fact, the spilled blood of the mistress of the house would be difficult. A lot more footwork was needed before the serologists at the crime lab could get down to business with their microscopes. Nevertheless, the noose of suspicion was tightening around Brian Jack's neck. A murder indictment against him was now almost inevitable.

The preliminary search of the residence had been wrapped up by 6:30 p.m. and the four detectives were anxious to hurry home. They all had wives and kids waiting for them. It was Christmas Eve and there were stockings to be filled.

The two forensic ferrets, Thompson and Luczenczyn, bagged the potential exhibits, locked the doors and left the house in darkness. It was 6:48. Soon they too would be at their firesides, enjoying a festive cup and sharing the joys of Christmas.

Still, the spirits of those who were concerned with the fate of Christine Jack had been dampened. There would be no family Christmas this year for little Kairsten and Adam. The hearts of a lot of tough cops ached for them.

Until he was satisfied that there was irrefutable evidence implicating Brian Jack, Staff Sergeant Ewatski could see little justification in keeping him caged up in the Remand Centre.

Ewatski was a straight cop. The rule book obsessed him. Being a Canadian Football League referee was but one of his many sidelines. He expected everybody to play by the rules, both on the field and off, just as he did.

Nobody had tried to pressure either him or Big John Speirs into securing Jack's release. It was their decision and they would make the arrangements. The fact that it was Christmas Eve had nothing to do with it. They would ensure that he slept in his own bed that night simply because it was the right thing for them to do.

On the off chance that some people might get the idea that Jack was being coddled by a couple of patsies, they could take heart. Both of these detectives had been major players in more than one high-profile murder conviction and several lesser ones as well.

The tall, subdued prisoner was escorted from his holding cell to the reception area where the two sergeants awaited his arrival. They stood and introduced themselves to Brian Gordon Jack.

Life is filled with unforeseeable twists and turns. Had Jack Ewatski and Brian Jack met under different circumstances, chances are they would have swapped football yarns and maybe even shared a pint or two.

There was an air of callous indifference about Jack on this occasion, however, as he half listened to what the two police officers were saying to him.

"Look, Brian," the staff sergeant said, "your house has been searched and several things have been seized, including blood-stained items. These will be compared with blood stains from the Blazer and with your wife's blood type. We figure it will take 48 hours and so you are going to be released from custody in the meantime, pending the results of the investigation."

There was no reply.

Speirs continued. "Your children have been apprehended by Child and Family Services and they have been placed in a temporary receiving home."

Again Jack said nothing.

Both policemen were somewhat startled that he failed to display the slightest emotion upon learning of Kairsten's and Adam's whereabouts.

Speirs cautioned him against attempting to locate the children upon his release.

Again there was no comment, just a languid affirmative nod of the head.

Prior to his release, it was decided that a watchful eye should be kept on the suspect. In some quarters there was apprehension that he would attempt to fly the coop. Due to manpower restrictions, however, there was little chance of maintaining discreet surveillance. Officers would be told to make no attempt to conceal themselves. Police vehicles would become commonplace in the vicinity of 170 Alburg Drive and Communications personnel would be alerted as to how to field telephone calls from anxious neighbours.

*Some circumstantial evidence is very strong,
as when you find a trout in the milk.*
—Henry David Thoreau

The Ste. Anne Connection

Paul St. Marie's eyes popped. Jim Hudrick did a double take. A third view of the vehicle had just flashed across the big screen.

"That's the Blazer we worked on about a week ago," the startled St. Marie announced with conviction.

The missing persons bulletin had been replayed following the late-night news.

"I know. I'll phone the city police right now," a tight-lipped Hudrick said.

The Speirs/Marshall team received the call at 11:45 that Tuesday night, just 48 hours after their prime suspect's deliverance from the lock-up.

On Wednesday morning, even before the birds were up, Detective Schinkel was down at the Remand Centre. He knew that Jack would have been photographed at the time of his admittance.

The mug shots of nine other dour faces were culled from the "dead file," and laid out on a table. They were all compatible with that of the suspected murderer. A gallery photopac was quickly assembled. It would be vital in discussion with the men from Ste. Anne.

❖ ❖ ❖ ❖ ❖

When Paul St. Marie or Jim Hudrick said they were going to do something, it was as good as done. They had arranged with Sergeants Speirs and Marshall to rendezvous with city police the following morning before nine o'clock.

And there they were, just as they had promised, sitting in Hudrick's tow truck which was parked at the curb beside the police garage.

Sergeant Harry Williams, grinning broadly, rapped on the driver's side window. His words of welcome were more akin to an expected greeting from the head of the local Chamber of Commerce than from a veteran homicide dick. But he had been at a pre-sunrise briefing with Speirs and Marshall and had gleaned a bit about the Ste. Anne connection.

The old sergeant appraised the two potential witnesses for the prosecution. These are the boys who are going to put the cheese in the trap for Brian Jack, his intuition told him.

It was always a treat for me to observe Harry Williams on the witness stand. Jurors hung on his every word. He spoke to them in confidence, as one old friend to another.

He was, first and foremost, a formidable investigator, but beyond that, a superlative showman. Often the more sagacious counsel for the defence would resign themselves to a Williams performance and forsake the right to cross-examine.

Lawrence Creighton, another intense young plain clothes constable (P.C.C.), stared intently at Schinkel's rogues' gallery.

"Great work, Loren," the neophyte chortled as he scooped up the photo lineup.

"Don't drop it," Schinkel cautioned. "Make sure you hand it directly to Sergeant Williams."

Creighton paused long enough to suggest that Schinkel pound salt up an orifice that would trigger instant discomfort. Then he bolted for the police garage.

Sergeant Williams tagged along behind as Jim Hudrick walked smartly towards the controversial Blazer, roped off in the southwest corner of the garage.

Up went the hood and down went Hudrick's head. Within seconds he stood, stretched and started nodding his head knowingly. He had recognized the antifreeze-diesel fuel mix spattered against the firewall.

"I still have some of that diesel oil in my garage," he told the sergeant.

It was then Paul St. Marie's turn. He grabbed Creighton's flashlight and nimbly slid under the vehicle. When finally he emerged, there was a look of triumph on his smudged but smiling face.

"It's the same one we worked on," he confided.

Methodically, as if they were casing it, the two mechanics worked their way around the Blazer. They stopped to examine the marks on the bumper, scuffed by the tow truck sling. Their heads bobbed in unison as they studied the rather rare square trailer hitch.

These men were prepared to swear on the Book of Life that this was, in fact, the vehicle they had attended to on the night of December 17.

Later that morning, in an interview room in the Crime Division offices, Detective Creighton handed the gallery photo lineup to Paul St. Marie. There was a youthful exuberance about this engaging young fellow. His impish grin, however, belied the tenacity of a bulldog just below the surface.

Brian Jack's photograph had been placed fourth from the top of the pac. St. Marie gave each of the first three photographs a cursory glance. He flipped the next one over, snatched it and slammed it down on the table in the blink of an eye.

"That's the dude," he hollered.

Detective Creighton followed through with the inevitable, "Are you absolutely sure?" St. Marie's reply was incisive.

"Yeah, I'm one hundred percent sure. I'm good with faces and license plates. That's the dude who had the truck trouble."

Ironically, among the fillers in the gallery pack was the face of a small-time hoodlum from Ste. Anne. Again, the identification was instantaneous and accurate.

Jim Hudrick was not so sure.

"I cannot make a positive identification," he told the police officers candidly.

"I was more concerned that night with fixing the truck than noticing the owner."

The bold affirmation, "That's the dude," was just the potent stimulus Harry Williams needed, however, to shift his ass into overdrive.

"Go get Hebert from Identification," he barked at Creighton. "Tell him to take a shot of the tow sling on Hudrick's truck. And tell him to bring his toothbrush. We leave for Ste. Anne in 15 minutes."

The old detective sergeant knew that it would take more than Paul St. Marie's word alone. If 12 jurors were to be left with no doubt that Brian Jack had been in the village of Ste. Anne on the night of December 17, other voices would have to be heard as well.

Jim Hudrick's tow truck rumbled across ice- and snow-encrusted roads, as the two mechanics bounced and jiggled all the way back to Ste. Anne.

By contrast, the three police officers lolled in the comfort of the midnight blue Crown Victoria during the satin-smooth ride to the village.

In my mind's eye, I can see Harry Williams now, reclining in the back seat like an overstuffed Charlie Chan, engrossed in his hypotheses concerning

Brian Jack. Harry was a disciple of the legendary Chinese detective and shared his wise philosophical reflections. He, too, acted on the assumption that if he could understand a man's character, he could predict his actions in any given circumstances.

Shortly before noon, two policemen and two stalwart citizens of Ste. Anne stood shivering in front of Jim Hudrick's 12-foot by 20-foot garage, while Constable Hebert scurried about taking measurements and photographs.

"That guy stopped the Blazer right about here," Hudrick stated while pointing to a spot just a step or two beyond the garage doors. "You can see that there was lots of room for him to have driven all the way in."

He then pointed to a blue, five-gallon plastic container where he stored antifreeze from a diesel motor.

"I poured at least two gallons of that stuff into the Blazer's rad," Hudrick said.

Meanwhile, Hebert filled two clean sealer jars with liquid from the plastic container and stashed them in the trunk of the police car.

The next location on the investigators' check list for scrutiny was out on the Trans-Canada Highway. An attempt would be made to gauge the distance east of the Ste. Anne cut-off where the mechanics last saw the Blazer on the night of December 17.

Again, the obliging Ste. Anne's men led the way. Within the hour the three police officers were huddled with Hudrick and St. Marie at the entranceway to the Love Nest Campground, some six miles east of Ste. Anne.

"This is close to the shoulder where the guy pulled over and paid us," Jim Hudrick told the assembled personnel. "We followed him down the road just about a mile and then we turned around and went home. It would have been around midnight.

"He was still traveling east on the Highway 1 and the Blazer was smoking badly from behind as the antifreeze in the oil was apparently burning. I told Paul that he wouldn't get very far with the truck in that condition. Paul said, 'I know.'

"If he had wanted to turn around, he could have gone about another four miles down the road to Richer and then turned around to head back to Winnipeg.

"There was no traffic on the road at that time of night."

❖   ❖   ❖   ❖   ❖

The Ste. Anne Connection

The most pressing reason for the Ste. Anne excursion was a viewing of the gallery pac by the proprietor of the local hotel and his staff.

While Williams and Creighton went off in search of Roger Pilloud and Brenda Appleyard, Hebert was busy focusing his lens on the hotel, the adjacent parking lot and on the neighbouring Co-op store.

Though the admonition from Holy Writ, "Seek and ye shall find," is very much a part of the Detectives' creed, neither of these two potential witnesses could be located.

"We'll come back tomorrow," the tenacious old sergeant muttered to no one in particular as he climbed into the back seat of the Crown Victoria.

❖ ❖ ❖ ❖ ❖

When the mug pac was handed to Roger Pilloud, Jack's photograph was third from the top.

Unhesitatingly, he extracted it from the series, stared at it momentarily and then said, "I think this is the guy, but I'd know him for sure if I saw him again."

Detective Creighton shuffled the deck and the killer's photo was now number five. Brenda Appleyard started to sift cautiously through the pac. Abruptly, dogmatically, she stated, "This is him for sure," while passing the photo of Brian Jack to Sergeant Williams. Then, ironically, just like Paul St. Marie, she pointed to the filler of the local bad apple and said, "I know this guy. He's from around here."

"Sure I know it was the night of December 17th when that guy came into the hotel looking for help," Ms. Appleyard emphatically told the detectives. "We had the 'Ken D' band playing in the bar on the 17th."

"You know, Lawrence," the old detective said to his younger partner as they stepped out onto Dawson Road, "when Brenda tells the jurors that Jack was in Ste. Anne on the night of December 17th, they will know that he was here."

❖ ❖ ❖ ❖ ❖

From the evidence that had already been gathered, the investigators were now satisfied to a moral certainty that Christine Jack was dead and that Brian Jack had killed her.

At 7:09 a.m. on January 3, 1989, Sergeants Speirs and Marshall arrested Brian Gordon Jack and charged him with the murder of his wife. He was then taken into custody.

> *When all is said and done, burial is the most common means of disposing of a body, the method preferred by killers as well as innocent, ordinary citizens.*
> —Dr. William R. Maples

A Futile Search

As the hours and days passed with no trace of the whereabouts of the body of Christine Jack, ugly rumours persisted. One of the more prevalent ones to be bandied about was that the body had been cremated. It was alleged that Brian Jack had a contact at a local mortuary. A brief investigation ensued and this supposition was discounted.

There is still a widely held belief that the killer dropped the body into a dumpster at the Salisbury House Restaurant at St. Anne's Road and Fermor Avenue, and that it had been transported from that location by a garbage-disposal unit to the Brady landfill site to be left to decompose among the tons and tons of rotting refuse.

Some were convinced that the body had fallen prey to carnivorous animals which abound in the area around Ste. Anne.

Sergeant Harry Williams studied the occurrence reports produced by the team of Paulishyn and Schinkel. He reflected upon Brian Jack's comment, "It will be all white now." These words became indelibly implanted in his brain. His sights for the next four months would be steadily trained upon the snow-packed environs of Ste. Anne and Hadashville, Manitoba, a nearby town.

In one of his rare but truthful utterances to police, their prime suspect had described the landscape with precision. It was all white, a white blanket of snow as far as the eye could see.

After having conferred with Jim Hudrick and Paul St. Marie in Ste. Anne on December 28, Sergeant Williams and Constable Creighton did a brief reconnaissance just off the Trans-Canada Highway near Ste. Anne. Fresh snowfalls had obliterated tire tracks and footprints. The snow was waist-deep in the places where they plodded. They would have to commandeer a helicopter to spearhead the search.

Their spirits were low as the two investigators headed home. The likelihood of discovering the body under these conditions was almost as remote as finding a marshmallow in an avalanche.

You can't keep a good man down, goes the old, familiar adage. Harry Williams confirmed it the following morning as he climbed into the Bell Ranger and buckled up.

The chopper, with Dan Stellman at the controls, lifted off the tarmac at St. Andrews Airport and headed southeasterly towards Ste. Anne.

During the short hop, the intrepid old sergeant briefed his hastily conscripted sidekick, Sergeant Garry Foster, an avid helicopter pilot himself.

As they hovered over the Love Nest Campground, their squinting eyes peered out upon the vast expanse of snow-clad prairie. The enormity of the task ahead would have stymied lesser men.

For three hours, Stellman flew in ever-increasing concentric circles well beyond the outskirts of Ste. Anne. This, the first of many aerial reconnaissances, yielded nothing more than a pair of very stiff necks.

Initial attempts to locate the body began with cursory treks on foot into the bush and fields around Ste. Anne. The depth of the snow was the greatest impediment to mobility. Frisky tracking dogs virtually swam through the drifts but their handlers could never keep up with them.

Snowmobilers and members of flying clubs were requested to keep a watchful eye.

Several air searches were undertaken between December and late April. Harry Williams personally logged 26 hours in the air.

The carcasses of deer, moose and dogs were sighted frequently. When investigators flew over the same terrain a short time later, more often than not the bodies had disappeared. The invariable conclusion was that the dead animals had been devoured by carnivores.

Throughout the course of the aerial explorations, the police would touch down each time they saw the corpses of slain animals. The old sergeant had an abiding conviction that they could offer clues to the murder victim's whereabouts.

By the end of the third week of April, the snow was melting and the ditches were beginning to fill with water.

On April 22, as the Bell Ranger fluttered over endless waterlogged fields, the dauntless Williams decided to abandon further airborne activity.

With the advent of spring, the time had come to launch a massive ground search. Big John Speirs handled the logistics with the deftness of a seasoned field commander.

Day after day he dispersed his troops over unfamiliar terrain.

More than 100 policemen, attuned to the clip-clop of their leather brogues on city sidewalks, grew accustomed to the slurp of slush-filled footwear.

They slogged their way along either side of the Trans-Canada Highway, all the way from Ste. Anne to Hadashville. Through soggy fields, gravel pits and low-lying areas of marsh and swampland, they trod relentlessly.

En route, they encountered bear and deer, coyotes and wolves in the dense underbrush. The bush was so thick in places that officers five feet apart couldn't see each other.

The magnitude of the search for the body of Christine Jack was unprecedented.

The tenacity of the seekers who braved the elements to reclaim her remains was awesome.

Despite the extensive and exhausting endeavours of scores of police officers, their mission ended in failure. Nevertheless, they would not give up hope.

Dr. Michael Baden, a former chief medical examiner for the City of New York, always stressed the fact that no burial is forever. Burial is only long-term storage, he said.

The renowned forensic anthropologist, Dr. William R. Maples, however, paints a more pessimistic picture.

> "A buried body," he observed, "can be devilishly difficult to find. In fact, except for the rare accident, buried bodies are seldom found unless someone confesses to their whereabouts. Even then, it may prove extraordinarily difficult to locate the actual grave because of changes in vegetation or terrain, or the confused state of mind of the individual who did the digging. 'It was dark. I couldn't really see. I think it was around here somewhere.' These are the vague directions you most often hear but if no one talks and the burial remains secret and the grave ages a bit, then finding a buried body is, in truth, the rarest of accidents. The killer who kills and buries the body without anyone's knowledge is safest from recovery of the remains. The more people present when the body was buried, the more likely it is to be found."[5]

You must look into people as well as at them.
—Lord Chesterfield

Profiles of the Protagonists

Perhaps a lucrative corporate practice would have been the wiser choice. Prosecuting murderers is hardly conducive to maintaining a serene disposition. With each successive day of trial, one's tolerance level is visibly diminished. Inevitably, the digestive system gets knocked out of kilter well before the jury is discharged.

By the time the verdict is delivered, I am always physically, mentally and spiritually debilitated. Well, nearly always. The first trial of Brian Gordon Jack turned out to be a rare exception.

It was the longest-running murder trial in Manitoba's history. Sworn in on September 10, 1990 the jurors were not relieved of their responsibilities until November 16. They remained cooped up inside the courthouse throughout the fairest days of autumn, doing their civic duty.

I well recall telling a skeptical colleague of mine just how much I had enjoyed every minute of this trial.

"Sure you did," I remember the doubting Thomas's retort. "Just like you enjoyed appearing before the rotund Gordie McTavish in night court while you prosecuted traffic violators."

George Dangerfield was a hard man to convince, but the simple truth is that I did enjoy every minute of this trial for a few very simple reasons, which will become readily apparent after a not altogether relevant reminiscence.

"It's not all one-sided," insisted a Queen's Bench Judge, affectionately known as "the Rabbit", as we strode along Winnipeg's tree-lined Broadway Avenue many years ago. We were both avid walkers and frequently fell into step on our way to work.

"You're always bitching," he said by way of mild rebuke, "when you don't draw the cream of the judicial crop to preside over your bloody murder trials. Has it ever occurred to you that we judges often have to abide inept lawyers? We don't always draw the cream of the defence bar, you know, or the fastest mounts from the Attorney General's stable, for that matter. Some of you guys would have been better off enrolling in Molar's Barber College or learning a trade," he fumed.

Suddenly it dawned on me. I, too, was out of the A.G.'s stable. Then and there I resolved to forego further judge-bashing. There would be no more judicial eulogies either, however few and far between, from that day forward. It would be up to legal historians, not me, to comment on their stewardship.

How ironic that within a decade I would have breached my pledge. Members of The Court of Appeal would become the targets of my unconscionable judge-bashing. Nevertheless, I still like to sing the praises of the worthy.

Chief Justice Benjamin Hewak was decidedly one of them. I was grateful that he, a former colleague in the Crown office, had assigned himself to the conduct of this trial.

Judges, like lawyers, come in a variety of shapes and sizes. The Chief Justice was built like a Chicago Bears corner linebacker. In his law school days, and afterwards as Crown counsel, he was known as "the Giant Buddha."

He had distinguished himself as a litigator long before his appointment to the Bench. His forte, however, was criminal law. His vast experience, both as Prosecutor and Defence counsel, was a boon when he came to grips with the countless legal entanglements that dominated this trial.

The Jack case, official Manitoba archives reveal, is one of only three murder trials in which the body was never found and the remains not positively identified. By coincidence, Chief Justice Hewak presided at all three trials.

Nobody in The Court of Queen's Bench was better equipped to handle this complicated case than the Giant Buddha himself. I guess it was the luck of the Irish that we got him on this one.

❖ ❖ ❖ ❖ ❖

If I ever get busted for a crime, any crime, I will rest easy if Richard Wolson undertakes my defence. His expertise in the criminal field is widely recognized. He is tenacious, cantankerous at times, but, to his undying credit, he plays by the code of rules established by the eighth Marquis of Queensbury in the middle of the 18th century.

My first impression of Richard, formed back in the fall of 1978, was a favourable one. He represented one of three louts indicted for attempted murder. The near-lethal weapon, believe it or not, was a toilet in the old Fort Garry Court, a once-fashionable apartment building adjacent to the prestigious Manitoba Club. It was the intention of the demented trio, by repeated flushings, to drown the hapless Armand Piché, as they secured his head inside the bowl.

Richard, a disciple of the redoubtable Harry Walsh, and I have had many skirmishes in the courtroom over the past 25 years. I cherish each and every one of them.

"Tiger" Wolson was another reason why I enjoyed the trial of Brian Jack.

❖ ❖ ❖ ❖ ❖

I have, and will always have, a warm spot in my heart for my co-counsel and long-time friend, Brian "Beanie" Kaplan. He brought his celebrated wit to the courtroom each and every day during this protracted and stressful trial.

His infectious humour again and again neutralized the tensions that inevitably mount while someone is being tried for murder. He was a tremendous hit with the ten ladies of the jury. Whenever he rose to examine a witness, their distressed features would give way to lingering smiles.

My associate chronically refuses to divulge the derivation of the name "Beanie" beyond acknowledging that he has been stuck with it for a long, long time. Apart from this non-disclosure and his personalized "Beanie" license plate, he is not at all eccentric. In fact, he is an otherwise totally rational being and an extremely accomplished advocate, as well.

"Beanie" contributed mightily to my enjoyment of this trial.

❖ ❖ ❖ ❖ ❖

Any one of the 46 witnesses called by the Prosecution would have been welcome at my table. Of the 16 police officers and 32 civilians who testified, the demeanour and disposition of all of them were admirable. With a mandatory roundup of so many people, along with all the attendant inconveniences, one would have expected the odd discordant note. There were none.

What a far cry from most murder trials where, among the members of the cast, the Neanderthal community is well represented.

We were blessed. No warrants were issued for absconding witnesses, nor were any declared hostile. The jury was favoured with a march past of good, reliable, concerned citizens whose only stake in the outcome of this trial was a just verdict.

Among the major witnesses for the Prosecution were two gracious young ladies, Cheryl MacMillan and Donna Mae Henry. They loved Christine Jack. Sharing their insights into her character proved invaluable to the triers of the facts. They attested, as well, to the troubles she had encountered during her final days.

During their testimony, moist eyes glistened in the gallery and in the jury box.

Cheryl, blond, vivacious and deeply devoted to her friend of 18 years, was 33, the same age as Christine. They were joint partners in Kinderspirit, a business enterprise engaged in the design and manufacture of children's clothing. Cheryl spoke of Chris's penchant for hard work, her conscientiousness and her dedication to her calling as a speech therapist.

Brian, whom she characterized as laid-back, carefree and irresponsible, had lost his business and was unemployed. Chris had become the breadwinner, she said, and the debts were piling up.

The long hours expended in pursuing her three jobs as homemaker, speech therapist and seamstress were taking their toll.

"Christine hadn't had a good night's sleep in the weeks before she disappeared," Cheryl told the jurors, "because her husband kept her up at night talking about their marital problems, and pleading with her to keep their marriage intact."

It was obvious to Cheryl that Christine was neglecting herself. She had lost weight and seemed sorely troubled.

"You've got to get away, Chris, even if it's just for a couple of days," Cheryl said to her. "Let's go to Grand Forks for the November eighteenth weekend. We will talk. It could be therapeutic."

It was during this brief excursion south of the border that Christine made contact with Earl Joseph Weber.

❖ ❖ ❖ ❖ ❖

"We were closer than sisters," testified Donna Henry, an attractive 32-year-old brunette, struggling to keep her voice and her emotions under control.

She had become involved in Kinderspirit and often joined in sewing sessions with Christine and Cheryl.

On December 10, just one week before Christine vanished, she and Chris were working on Christmas orders. It was on that occasion that Christine confided that she was terrified of Brian and didn't know what to do. He had "pinned her down" the previous evening for ten ti fifteen minutes when she had broached the subject of their separating.

The jurors sat transfixed as Donna, fighting valiantly to hold back the tears, told of the startling request that her friend had made.

"If anything happens to me, Donna, would you take care of the kids for me?"

❖   ❖   ❖   ❖   ❖

The Jankovecs and the Reiters, Christine Jack's parents, had been friends for 25 years. There was a very special bond between Lidijia Jankovec and Christine.

"Christine always called me Tante Lidijia," Mrs. Jankovec said. "Tante is German for aunt."

A week or so before the trial, I drove out to her flower-laden home in Selkirk so that we could review her anticipated testimony.

I sank down on the chesterfield in her tastefully decorated living room. Her soft voice, with lingering Teutonic overtones, was pleasing to the ear. As she spoke, I took copious notes. She possessed an inherent sense of what was relevant and she didn't ramble. At the conclusion of her discourse, I couldn't think of one single question that needed to be answered.

"Christine married Brian about eight years ago," she said. "I found out about a month ago that they were having problems in their marriage. Brian had lost his business and wasn't working. He would just do whatever he wanted to do, whenever he felt like it. He'd go hunting and fishing and do other things, while Christine would have to get up early, look after the kids and go to work.

"I phoned Christine on December 5 or 6. She said that Brian was home and she couldn't talk then. She phoned me two or three days later, about 10:30 in the morning. She told me about the problems she was having with him.

"She said that the night before, Brian had climbed on top of her and pinned her on the bed, because he wanted to talk to her but she didn't want to listen. She was crying and I thought that he had hit her. I asked her if he had hit her and hurt her and if he had, I told her that she should call the police.

"She said no, he hadn't hit her, but that he had thrown her on the bed and had pinned her down so that she would listen to him. That was when I told her that if things got worse, she should pack up and bring her children to come and stay with me for a few days.

"Around December 10, I again talked to Christine on the phone. She told me once more about how bad it was at home and that she wanted to get a legal separation.

"I was very worried about Christine and the children, so I called around 9 a.m. on Saturday, December 17. Brian answered. I had intended to visit. However, Brian said that they were all going to a Christmas party.

"I spoke briefly with Christine, too. I asked her if they were still coming for Boxing Day dinner and she said, 'Yes,' and that they were all looking forward to it. This is the last time I talked to her," she said as tears started flowing.

I suggested that we take a break then, or perhaps continue our preparation for the trial another day. She left the room visibly upset.

While I sat contemplating my departure, I heard her bustling about in the kitchen. A few minutes later, she returned, carrying a tray. We drank coffee and I feasted on superb apple strudel.

Is it really necessary to clog the record with all of these superfluous details? No, it is merely a personal reminiscence of a very sweet and compassionate human being who ended up being one of the more formidable witnesses with whom Richard Wolson had to contend.

By now, she had regained her composure and was anxious to carry on.

"It was at 5:10 the following morning when I was awakened by the ringing of the telephone," she continued. "I have both the phone and a clock by my bed and I noticed the time. It was Brian. His voice was shaky, like he was crying. He said that he and Christine had had a fight the night before and that they were screaming at each other. He said she had asked him to leave but that he had refused because he had no place to go. The screaming continued. Then she grabbed her purse, her keys and her green coat, went to the Blazer and drove off. This is exactly what he told me," Mrs. Jankovec sighed.

"Brian said he was very worried because Christine hadn't returned and he had no idea where she had gone. He asked if she was with me or if I knew where she had gone. Later that day I telephoned Christine's mother in New Jersey on the off chance that she had heard from her daughter. She hadn't, so I passed along to her what Brian had told me.

"I have had numerous telephone chats with Brian. There is still no news about Christine's whereabouts."

I had stayed longer than I intended and Mrs. Jankovec was showing signs of weariness. As I rose to leave, she took both of my hands. The tears reappeared.

"It's just not like Christine to go somewhere and leave the kids and not tell anyone. I just don't know what has happened. I'm afraid."

Her anguish over Christine's fate and her sympathy for Veletei and Stephan Reiter were deep-rooted. Her love for Kairsten and Adam, so freely expressed, and her grave concern for their well-being as they tried to cope without their mother was mirrored in her face.

As I drove back into the city, an uncharacteristic sadness came over me.

❖ ❖ ❖ ❖ ❖

Lidijia Jankovec was summoned to testify on Thursday, October 4, 1990. A month had elapsed since our meeting. She was nervous and anxious to testify and be gone. But as her evidence unfolded, she relaxed. She spoke clearly, coherently and omitted nothing of significance. She faltered only once, while she told the mesmerized jurors of one of her last conversations with Christine Jack:

"I asked Christine whether there was any hope for the marriage. 'There is no more love, there is not even hate; there is nothing—emptiness,' she replied."

❖ ❖ ❖ ❖ ❖

As Lord Chesterfield said, "You must look into people as well as at them."

And isn't that what jurors do?

And isn't that what these jurors did? They looked at Tante Lidijia and Cheryl and Donna Mae and they looked into them and they evaluated them. And they accepted the cumulative effect of their testimony. Christine Jack would never have willfully abandoned her children, never as long as she drew a breath.

> *I told him it was law logic—an artificial system of reasoning, exclusively used in courts of justice, but good for nothing else.*
> —President John Quincy Adams

Mr. Weber

Earl Joseph Weber was a tall man, well-built, and moved with the gait of a guardsman. Just three years younger than Brian Jack, he bore a resemblance to him in the same large frame with no excessive baggage, the same regular features, the same moustache, the same receding hairline. One might have experienced difficulty in determining which was which, even at a short distance.

He was a resident of Grand Forks, North Dakota, and a civilian employee of the United States Armed Forces.

Earl Weber could shed no light on how Christine Jack was slain or what was done with her body.

Nothing he could say, absolutely nothing, would advance the case for the Prosecution. No two mortals were more cognizant of this fact than Brian Kaplan and I were.

But by dint of the law's illogic, we were boxed into a corner. At all costs, Earl Weber had to be called as a witness by the Prosecution. His absence from the witness stand could have raised reasonable doubt in the mind of just one juror, which would scuttle any chance of a conviction for Jack. Weber's evidence was crucial.

But he was an American citizen. There was no way we could compel him to appear. A subpoena issued out of the Court of Queen's Bench had no more force and effect south of the forty-ninth parallel than a discarded gum wrapper.

Earl Weber was a man of honour. He would be available, he told us unhesitatingly, whenever we wanted him in court.

For the best part of the juridical day, Wednesday, October 3, the ever-courteous Weber was subjected to a barrage of questions from counsel both for the Crown and for the Defence.

Never, in my experience, was so much irrelevant testimony foisted upon a jury. It had about as much probative value as an ostrich egg to an ant. Brian Jack's guilt or innocence would not be determined by the utterances of Earl Weber. The ever-vigilant Kaplan and I were vitally aware of this when we made our decision to call him. We had no option.

"Sure you did," I hear another doubting Thomas cry. "You guys were the prosecutors. You had the discretion to decide which witnesses to call."

Had it not been for what I will always regard as an ill-conceived judgment of the Supreme Court, Earl Weber would never have been asked to testify.

There is no doubt that, in a criminal case involving an indictable offence, there has always existed a duty on the part of the Crown to sit down with opposing counsel and make full, fair and timely disclosure of all relevant facts. Only recently, however, did that obligation include delivering up to the Defence each and every investigative report.

When I was a young, aggressive Crown attorney, I guarded all occurrence reports as if they were the crown jewels.

I can still see the ill-fated, bold, purple letters of the warning stamped on the face sheets of the reports—"Property of The Winnipeg Police Department—return to Crime Division."

The Crown attorney, entrusted with a major crime report from the General Investigation Section of the R.C.M.P. received a reminder that this document was for his eyes only.

Today, and at Jack's trial, by virtue of the 1975 judgment of the Supreme Court in the case of *Regina v. Caccamo*,[6] woe betide the Crown attorney or any lawman who withholds anything revealed during the police probe from the Defence.

The revelation of the existence of Earl Weber could easily have boomeranged. What a glorious opportunity for an astute Defence counsel to weave a web of suspicion and create a climate of doubt surrounding the demise of Christine Jack.

Ensconsed in my den at night while preparing for trial, I was haunted by the shrill voice of Richard Wolson, imploring the jurors to release his client from this illegitimate bondage:

"There is no more love—nothing, emptiness," he remonstrates. "In her anguish, she seeks solace in the arms of a former lover. The spark is rekindled. Who is to say that she has not found sanctuary through collaboration with Weber? I caution you: There is not a tittle of proof that Christine Jack is dead."

There was no choice for us. Either we produced Earl Weber to testify, or we faced a very real possibility that Brian Jack would walk.

❖ ❖ ❖ ❖ ❖

During an interview with the police a week after the disappearance of Christine Jack, Cheryl MacMillan casually mentioned having telephoned Earl Weber, an ex-boyfriend of Chris's who lived in Grand Forks. She wanted him to know that Chris was missing, she said.

The investigators, hungry for any scrap of information they could get, arranged a meeting with Weber. They were surprised at his unexpected candour and cooperation.

"I met Chris back in 1973, when we were both students at the University of North Dakota," he told them.

"How serious was our relationship? Well, we were engaged twice. I broke off the first engagement but we got back together. We had even set a date for the wedding. Well, after Chris graduated, she went back to Canada. This time, it was she who terminated our engagement."

Though they went their separate ways, married and had families, neither had forgotten the other. "During the summer of 1988, I called Chris just to see how she was doing," the affable North Dakotan recalled. "I gathered that she felt uncomfortable talking to me. I gave her my two phone numbers, and told her that if she ever needed a friend to talk to, I would be there. After that, I told myself that I would not call her again.

"It was on November fourteenth that she telephoned to say that she was coming to town the following weekend with a girlfriend and was wondering if we could meet. I said, 'Yes.'"

I think back to the time when my good friend Richard Wolson wandered aimlessly about in the wilderness until—until, like the manna miraculously supplied to the Israelites, the police report containing the Weber revelations fell into his lucky lap.

"When did you meet her?" the police wanted to know.

"Friday, November 18, at 10:00 p.m."

"Where?"

"At Chi-Chi's. She had contacted me at work. We established the time and place."

"Who was present when you met?"
"Just Chris, Cheryl MacMillan and I."
"How did Christine appear to you?"
"Normal, quiet, shy."
"How long did you stay at Chi-Chi's?"
"Until about midnight."
"Did you go anywhere after Chi-Chi's?"

"Yes, Chris and I went to the university campus. Cheryl had gone back to the motel about 45 minutes prior to us going out to the university. We went in my truck."

"Why did you go there?"

"It was a place we had walked around whe we were dating, and we just went there to talk and walk around."

"What did you discuss?"

"We discussed our lives, from the time we had separated until now."

"Was there any physical attraction?"

"We held hands, we held each other, and we kissed."

"How passionately?"

"It wasn't a passionate kiss."

"What, specifically, did you discuss about your lives?"

"Chris told me about her marriage and how things weren't going all that well and hadn't for quite some time. She said that she didn't think things were going to change."

The questioning went on incessantly, covering a wide range of topics:

"Did Christine speak at all about her children?"

"She showed me a picture of them and told me about them. I also showed her a picture of mine. Typical parent talk."

❖ ❖ ❖ ❖ ❖

The day following Earl Weber's testimony, tabloid-type headlines, calculated to titillate, beckoned the reader:

CHRISTINE JACK MEETS SECRETLY WITH EX-FIANCÉ

Then a sub-headline:

Met him month before vanishing

An alert staff photographer got a dandy shot of the husky American as he left the Law Courts Building. This picture accompanied the story, with the heading::

MISSING WOMAN TOLD EX-FIANCÉ OF MARITAL WOES

The sub-headline:

Court hears of meetings in U.S.

prefaced a lurid account. It, too, featured Weber's photograph.

The reports in both daily newspapers confirmed that Earl Weber was as forthright with the Court as he had been with police.

The jurors heard about the walk down memory lane, the acknowledgment that "some of the old spark remained," the hand-holding and the caresses.

Only once during a vigorous cross-examination did Earl Weber exhibit mild irritation. No, he had not seen Christine Jack since the Grand Forks visit, and, no, he hadn't been in Winnipeg around the time she disappeared.

❖ ❖ ❖ ❖ ❖

Two weeks later, Brenda Louise Appleyard, the waitress from the Ste. Anne Hotel, took the witness stand.

It was while Brian Kaplan was ushering her through her examination that something she said raised more than one eyebrow in the jury box.

She had been approached the day before by Mr. Wolson. He had shown her a picture of a man. She identified him as Christine Jack's former fiancé, a man whose picture she had seen in the media, she said.

Ste. Anne Hotel owner Roger Pilloud testified that the Defence lawyer showed him Earl Weber's picture before court.

"At first I thought it was Mr. Jack. After that, when I really looked at it, I knew it wasn't."

❖ ❖ ❖ ❖ ❖

The late Mr. Justice John Sopinka of the Supreme Court of Canada was an outstanding athlete in the days of his youth. He played in the Canadian

Football League on those same fields where Brian Jack had scrimmaged.

An old football pro like His Lordship would have seen the necessity of level ground on the gridiron.

It startled me, then, that he had failed to recognize the tilt in the field of criminal law so steeply sloped in favour of the Defence.

In the early nineties a judgment of the Supreme Court, written by Mr. Justice Sopinka, stated in part:

> ...the fruits of the investigation which are in the possession of counsel for the Crown are not the property of the Crown for use in securing a conviction but the property of the public to be used to ensure that justice is done. In contrast, the Defence has no obligation to assist the Prosecution and is entitled to assume a purely adversarial role toward the Prosecution."[7]

The mandatory obligation to reveal the identity of Earl Weber came with a hefty price tag. Apart from the inconvenience inflicted upon him, there were increased costs, wasted court time and potential mischief to the case for the Prosecution.

Kaplan and I did what we had to do. We too were the victims of law logic, that artificial system of reasoning, exclusively used in courts of justice but good for nothing anywhere else.

> *You have really done very well indeed. It is true that
> you have missed everything of importance...*[8]
> —Sherlock Homes

A Case of Mistaken Identity

The possibility that Christine Jack had dined alone in the Rib Room of Winnipeg's Charter House Hotel six days after her sudden disappearance struck Brian Kaplan and me as being somewhat remote.

Hotel waitresses Shirley Garbutt and Donna Pike insisted that they had seen her there.

The likelihood of Christine Jack surfacing in the Rib Room and dining on crab, we concluded, was as improbable as spotting a hammerhead shark in the Charter House pool.

We felt no moral or legal obligation to call these two ladies as witnesses. Their testimony could no more assist the jury in its deliberations than the testimony of Earl Weber himself.

A most persuasive Richard Wolson convinced Chief Justice Hewak, however, that the Court should call them to the stand.

By virtue of the Court's initiative, the Defence did not have to subpoena them as witnesses.

When counsel for an accused person elects to call no evidence at the conclusion of the case for the Prosecution, he reserves the right to address the jury last. This is seen as a decided advantage by most Defence counsels, a notion I have yet to comprehend.

❖ ❖ ❖ ❖ ❖

On Tuesday morning, November 6, 1990, almost two years after Christine Jack had been reported missing, Shirley Garbutt was invited by the Chief

A Case of Mistaken Identity

Justice to tell the jurors what she knew about the matter before the Court.

"A woman wearing dark clothing came into the dining room on December 23, 1998 between 5:00 and 6:00 p.m. She was the only patron and she stayed for about 45 minutes," Mrs. Garbutt stated.

"Although I didn't serve her, I noticed that she ordered an expensive crab dinner and sent it back uneaten. I had never seen this woman before, but I got a good look at her face and I noticed that she looked upset.

"A day or two later there was a picture in the *Sun* showing the missing Christine Jack and right away I told my husband that this was the woman who had been in the dining room."

Mrs. Garbutt described the stranger as being five feet, eight inches tall with shoulder-length, light brown hair, straighter than Christine Jack's was in the photograph.

"When I first saw the photo in the newspaper, there was not much doubt in my mind that the woman was Christine Jack. My first reaction was that this was the woman I saw," she said.

Ironically, Mrs. Garbutt failed to notify police of her observations or suspicions for at least seven days, between seven and ten days, she calculated.

After having shepherded the first Charter House waitress through her testimony, His Lordship informed counsel that he would permit cross-examination.

The nimble Kaplan moved immediately to a position close to the witness box. There was an uncharacteristic edge to his voice.

"The reason you waited seven to ten days after you saw the picture in the paper was that you weren't completely sure. Was there some doubt in your mind?"

The question seemed to take the witness by surprise. She said that her "first reaction" upon seeing the newspaper photo was that it was the same person, but that she hadn't "interacted" with the woman in the dining room.

"I was initially reluctant to get involved with the police and later spoke to Donna Pike, the waitress who had served the woman," Shirley Garbutt confessed.

She testified that she and Donna agreed that the woman shown in the newspaper was the same person who had been in the dining room and that they had talked to the hotel manager about her. He told them not to get involved, she claimed.

However, she decided eventually to call the police. She did so but they never called back, she said.

Crown counsel asked her whether she didn't think that her information was important enough to warrant a second call, considering the fact that Brian Jack had been charged with killing his wife.

"Didn't you think that what you knew could possibly saved someone from a charge of murder?" Kaplan asked.

"Yes, I did," Garbutt replied defiantly. "And I wondered why I wasn't contacted or interviewed by the police," she snapped.

"Why didn't you call the police again after you learned that the officers had talked to Donna Pike?" Kaplan pressed.

"I called them initially," she replied caustically. "It is the duty of the police to follow up on information provided by citizens. I thought they would cover all leads. Obviously they don't," she scoffed.

This was the only day of the trial which ended on a sour note.

❖ ❖ ❖ ❖ ❖

The following morning, at ten o'clock sharp, Donna Pike settled into a chair on the witness stand. She was positioned about six feet to the right of the Chief Justice and no more than a car length away from the jury box.

The judge's boyish smile and the deference he showed her seemed to put her at ease in those unfamiliar surroundings.

Throughout the course of her lengthy testimony, she exhibited none of the impertinence of the previous witness. Her distinguishing characteristic, however, was her uncompromising stance. She served Christine Jack in the Rib Room of the Charter House Hotel on December 23, 1988, and that was that.

Pike told the jurors that the woman appeared to be about five feet, eight inches tall with dirty-blond, streaked hair and that she wore a fire-engine red coat throughout dinner. The woman was curt and upset. Then she recollected:

> She came into the Rib Room about 6:00 p.m. and for a while she was the only customer. She ordered a crab dinner with a salad and a Caesar drink. What stood out in my mind was that she paid 25 dollars for the meal but didn't touch any of it. She paid for it in cash…

I am getting a little long in the tooth now. Things don't snap into focus as fast as they used to. Still, my memory is as crystal clear as it was in my heyday as I replay her testimony and remember the look on the faces of the jurors, which bespoke their incredulity.

For almost two months, they had been concentrating on the evidence of 46 Crown witnesses, many of whom knew Christine Jack intimately. They had formed their own impressions of Kairsten and Adam's mother. They had learned of her fierce devotion to her children, her dedication to her profession, her Kinderspirit enterprise and her frugality in order to make ends meet.

A solitary seafood dinner and Caesar cocktail in one of the city's five-star restaurants was incompatible with Christine Jack's lifestyle during the 1988 Christmas season.

Pike informed the jurors that she had seen a picture of the missing Christine Jack in the newspaper the very next morning. She was positive that this was the woman who had been at the hotel the evening before.

"It was definitely the same woman," she said. "I phoned the police immediately and left them my telephone number as well as that of my parents, with whom I would be visiting for a week."

After having learned that Brian Jack had been charged with his wife's murder, the waitress said that she was surprised that no one at the police had contacted her.

"I didn't call the police again," she said.

Kaplan asked Pike, who was much mellower than the preceding day, if she was aware of the massive search the police had conducted for the missing woman. She acknowledged that she was well aware of it.

"To you, I assume, Mrs. Pike, they were going on a wild goose chase?" Kaplan suggested.

"Right," she replied crisply.

He then asked her why, if she was aware of the murder charge and the extensive search for the body, she didn't again call the police.

"They had my number. If they wanted to talk to me, they could have called me," she retorted.

"Were you prepared to let an innocent man remain charged with murder?" Kaplan persisted.

"Well, no," Pike replied unconvincingly.

"But you didn't call again?"

"No."

My associate, a student of Isadore Levinter's grasshopper method of cross-examination, abruptly jumped to another topic.

"Would you have been concerned had you known that Christine Jack didn't own a red coat or had never streaked her hair?" Kaplan demanded.

"She could have done anything in the six days she was missing," Pike muttered with very little conviction.

Trials & Errors: The People vs. Brian Gordon Jack

❖ ❖ ❖ ❖ ❖

The Court, acceding to the request of Crown counsel, called Mr. George Gershman as the final witness in the trial. He was the general manager of the Charter House Hotel.

Gershman vehemently disputed the claim of his two waitresses, Shirley Garbutt and Donna Pike, that the one diner was Christine Jack.

He had seen Mrs. Jack's picture in the newspapers. He stated most emphatically that she was not the person he had seen in the dining room.

❖ ❖ ❖ ❖ ❖

Instances of false identification are commonplace in the annals of true crime. As soon as the media had reported that O.J. Simpson and Al Cowlings were on the run, Los Angeles police were deluged with phone calls from tipsters. One reported having seen Simpson with a former teammate dining in a French restaurant in Santa Monica; another had observed him, resplendent in a white suit, eating alone in a Winner's Restaurant in Atlanta, Georgia.

Extreme caution must be exercised in evaluating the testimony of the tipster. The Brian Jack jurors were vigilant. They were also unanimous. Shirley Garbutt and Donna Pike had been mistaken.

> *Let thy speech be short, comprehending much in few words.*
> —Ecclesiasticus XXXII.8

Crown Counsel's Closing Address

As I rose to speak, I reaffirmed my commitment to spare the jury the histrionics.

This time there was no murder weapon, no knife or gun or axe to shamelessly flaunt while slyly seeking a gain of a few subliminal yards. These jurors, I reminded myself, were sufficiently inflamed without any contribution on my part.

During the ten-week trial, 46 witnesses gave evidence on behalf of the prosecution. The testimony of each and every one was of vital significance in the development of the case against Brian Jack.

For those of us who still have an abiding faith in trial by jury, heavy reliance is placed on the capacity of the 12 jurors to collectively recall and evaluate all of the evidence.

The final oration, then, is relatively succinct. But not this time.

Vaguely familiar with the teachings of the 16th century French theologian and prolific writer François Fenelon, I had initially vowed to adhere to his wise counsel. It would deter me from straying too far off the path of brevity:

> "The more you say," he warned, "the less people remember. The fewer the words, the greater the profit."

Sound advice indeed, particularly when one contemplates the limited attention span of each of the triers of the facts.

The natural inclination to rehash the testimony of the major witnesses and to allude to the testimony of the minor ones is usually resisted during the closing addresses of counsel. The jurors have already heard the evidence. Furthermore, there are other issues to be dealt with during the precious moments allocated to the adversaries' summations.

I slept fitfully during the last week of trial. Tranquility finally overtook me when I eventually concluded that there was far too much at stake to opt for a cursory review. Time was no longer of the essence.

It was past 11:00 a.m. when the court rose for the morning recess, a quaint euphemism for a fast cup of coffee and a visit to the comfort station. I had been speaking for more than an hour.

Sixty more minutes passed until it dawned on me that people would be getting hungry. It was well past noon.

His Lordship breathed an ill-concealed sigh of relief when I respectfully suggested this would be an appropriate time to break for lunch.

Napoleon said that victory belongs to the most persevering. This bold assertion may well be so on the battlefield. It remained to be seen how applicable it was in the courtroom.

As the jurors resumed their places after a two-hour respite, I scanned them. They all appeared to have been well-fed and watered and in no way impaired by the morning session. In fact, as juries go, I found this one to be surprisingly docile.

I was on my feet again for well over an hour. Mercifully, the Chief Justice intervened and we recessed for another 20 minutes.

It has been said that the secret of being tiresome is in telling everything. I appreciate this truism. No closing address of mine in previous murder trials had ever exceeded 80 minutes.

It was 3:50 p.m. as we started in to the home stretch. I felt uneasy. Perhaps I should have heeded the admonition from Ecclesiasticus in Holy Writ and let my speech be short, comprehending much in few words. I prayed that my verbosity was not going to cost us dearly. When the checkered flag was finally waved, my closing address to the jury totalled more than four hours.

> *Resort is had to ridicule only when reason is against us.*
> —President Thomas Jefferson

Damn the Prosecution

The voice of Richard Wolson rose in righteous indignation as he pointed an accusatory finger at both Crown counsel and the police. This tack was as inevitable as were the hushed tones Richard reserved for his plea for the jurors' sympathetic understanding of the plight of his innocent client.

In many of his pleas, the celebrated American trial lawyer Clarence Darrow directed his ire against an individual. It might be the prosecutor, a witness for the opposing side, or the complainant. This tactic, in plea after plea, was one of Darrow's favourite means of making the jury sympathize, not only with the defendant, but with any man who is under brutal scrutiny for his motives and frailties.[9]

I have been under the impression for years that my learned friend Richard Wolson keeps a copy of *Attorney for the Damned*, Darrow's trial memoirs, on his bedside table.

❖ ❖ ❖ ❖ ❖

My adversary bowed deferentially to the judge and then to the jurors.

His voice was as sombre and subdued as if he were speaking to a family in mourning.

He began:

"May it please My Lord, ladies and gentlemen:

"Brian Jack's love for Christine, Adam and Kairsten is undeniable, and about that there can be no doubt. He tried everything within his power to keep that family together because of that love.

"Yesterday Crown counsel urged you to convict Brian Jack for the murder of Christine.

"Do you think that he would kill the love of his life, his rock, his strength, his reason for being? And, as importantly, do you think that he would take Christine, the wonderful mother, from the other loves of his life, Adam and Kairsten?

"That is not the man we have heard about in this courtroom. That is not Brian Jack. But, yet, for the past 23 months, Brian Jack has lived a nightmare.

"Since December 17, 1988, when Christine Jack left 170 Alburg Drive, Brian tried to put the pieces together, hoping she would return. And then he was charged with her murder.

"He has been put under a microscope, his actions examined in minute detail. And while he has been subjected to this treatment, people saw Christine Jack here in Winnipeg. And that evidence was suppressed."

Abruptly, the voice of tranquility was displaced by the rasp of a buzz saw.

"Mr. Jack is presumed innocent, but while he has that presumption of innocence, every fact has been slanted against him. The police," Wolson sneered, "through their one-sided, inadequate and negligent investigation have tried to reconcile every fact with his guilt. And the Crown has taken those facts and have asked you to convict Brian Jack.

"It's enough," he snapped. "Stop. Look at the evidence. Brian Jack is not guilty. Stop this injustice."

Counsel paused just long enough for his anger to abate. Then, calmly and with conviction, he said:

"As His Lordship told you, you are the judges of the facts, and the terrible and final responsibility of determining the guilt or innocence of Brian Jack rests with you.

"What an important decision! How often in your lives will your decision affect another so much as yours will affect Brian Jack? His future is in your hands.

"I know that you will discharge that responsibility in an honest and fair way. I appreciate, and Mr. Jack appreciates, the careful attention you have given the evidence in this case."

Next, Richard donned his professorial robes and delivered his introductory course in the history and evolution of the jury system. He had been a sessional lecturer in law for many years and was always well received.

"Since back in September," he said, "September tenth to be exact, you have been involved in a very serious and important task. You have been involved in the jury system of justice. It's not a new system, it's not a system that developed five or ten years ago, but hundreds of years ago in Great Britain. And we have seen fit to adopt this as our system, and we guard it jealously because it lies at the basis, the foundation of freedom in this country."

He extolled the virtues of a system that relies on the verdict of 12 men and women as it more closely approximates the truth than the verdict of one man alone.

The professor was nearing the end of his discourse on the efficacy of the unanimous verdict when, with the dexterity of a magician, he switched from academic gown to barrister's robe.

"Now, during my address, if I fail to mention some points that you think are important," he implored, "raise them in the jury room. Fight for Brian Jack.

"Do something the police didn't do. Give him a fair trial, as I know you will."

Like a squall, the high pitch and the edge in the voice quickly subsided. Richard deftly slipped back into his cap and gown and returned to the classroom. The presumption of innocence and the doctrine of reasonable doubt were about to be addressed.

"At the beginning of this case," he reminded the assembly, "the Chief Justice told you that we have rules in our system of justice. Some have referred to them as the golden rules. They apply to everyone in this country; not just to Brian Jack, but to everyone.

"The golden rules mean that Brian Jack is presumed innocent, as we all are before the law. Brian has nothing to prove. And the rule goes on to state that it's for the Crown to prove guilt, and to prove it beyond a reasonable doubt. There is no onus on Brian. He stands innocent before you."

The jurors would learn more about what constitutes a reasonable doubt, and the standard of proof to be applied, before Richard Wolson left the lecture hall and returned to the courtroom.

❖ ❖ ❖ ❖ ❖

"Well, what is the evidence in this case?" the effusive Defence counsel asked. "We have heard a great deal about Brian Jack and Christine Jack. I'd like to review the profile of Brian Jack.

"As the Crown conceded, a well-educated man. Bachelor of Arts degree from a university in the States, majoring in economics and physical education. He has run a number of businesses here in the City of Winnipeg. At one point, he ran a number of Pro Shops and the Fit Stop. He had his own business on St. Anne's Road. He has been a substitute teacher at schools here in this city. He ran for school trustee. And you know that he was looking for work. He had an interview with the tourism department of the provincial government. A well-educated man, an intelligent man. And I'd ask you to keep that in mind, an intelligent man.

"Despite that, however, he had a speech problem. You heard about it. When he talked, he would say, 'Ah, ah, ah.' Those words would be interjected in his speech."

This was not Richard Wolson's finest hour despite a valiant attempt to explain away the ums and the ahs and the long pauses. The jumbled jargon to which the three investigators, Schinkel, Paulishyn and Hatcher, had attested had not been forgotten by the triers of the facts.

Counsel pressed the point.

"Patricia Gagné knew Brian Jack for a number of years. That's how he talked.

"Annette Clay knew Brian Jack for eight or nine years. That's how Brian talked."

I well recall the look of pained incredulity which creased the faces of several jurors when Defence counsel said:

"Remember the testimony of Officers Paulishyn and Schinkel. That's how Brian talked. Even when he was talking about something as innocuous or as unimportant as background, where he went to school, that's how Brian Jack talked."

To the best of my knowledge, it was Mr. Wolson, and he alone, who had diagnosed his client's blithering as a "speech problem." Certainly there was no evidence before the Court that Christine Jack, a registered speech therapist, had ever treated her husband professionally.

❖ ❖ ❖ ❖ ❖

A little vignette of a very personal nature would have dispelled further doubt about Brian Jack's capacity to speak coherently. But first an explanatory note. It is not my practice to record the times when, or places where, I go to respond to nature's call. Mid-morning, May 10, 1989, was a rare exception, however. This was the day when the Jack preliminary inquiry got off the ground. The ever-punctual Judge Howard Collerman blew the whistle for the kickoff at ten o'clock sharp. Court recessed at 11:15.

I made my way to the washroom adjacent to the courtroom door. My arrival time was 11:16.

"How are you doing?" boomed the voice of the interloper who had attended the comfort station after me and had taken up a position to my immediate left.

Wrongfully assuming for the moment that it was my droll associate, "Beanie" Kaplan, I was about to deliver a brilliant riposte like, "How am I doing what?" when my eyes fleetingly strayed.

To my astonishment, it wasn't Brian Kaplan. It was the other Brian, Brian Jack. I couldn't believe my eyes, or my ears for that matter. He started chattering away to me like I was a long-lost buddy.

I didn't get it. I still don't. Within the preceding half hour, he sat with his lawyers at the Defence table. He heard me, one of his prosecutors, address Judge Collerman.

I informed the Court that the evidence which the Crown intended to lead during the ensuing several days would be more than sufficient to satisfy a reasonable jury, properly instructed, that Brian Gordon Jack had indeed murdered his wife.

As I said, I was his prosecutor, not his squash partner. Nevertheless, this didn't seem to faze him. He followed me out into the corridor, talking all the while.

On a subsequent occasion during a recess, I remained seated in the courtroom, conversing with the Clerk of the Court. Jack sat down in a chair near us and joined in the conversation. It was an awkward situation.

❖ ❖ ❖ ❖ ❖

It has been said that one of the tools of the lawyer's trade is his effective use of words. I have a keen ear for the spoken word.

This much I know is true: Jack no more had a speech problem than did Wolson or Kaplan or I.

Counsel then set about the task of trying to convince the jury that Brian Jack was not a man of violence, but that he was a nice, mild, unobtrusive fellow who would be loath to swat a mosquito or trample on a potato bug.

The impassioned defender's voice climbed higher on the scale.

"Brian Jack is not the cold, calculating, diabolical killer that Crown counsel invited you to find from the evidence," he chided indignantly, "because that isn't the evidence."

"And, yes, he is right. I'll mention that to you over and over again, because there is no evidence of that. That's a fanciful thought by a skillful, articulate prosecutor, one of the best."

Bent on embellishing the notion that his client was one so gentle, meek and mild, counsel borrowed from the testimony of Annette Clay.

"'Not loud,' Annette told you. She told you that despite his size, because he is a large man—despite that, she said to you, her words not mine, 'A lovable teddy bear-type fellow, a nice fellow.'

"His personality?" Jack's lawyer queried as if someone else had posed the question. "Not aggressive. That's not the voice of his lawyer talking. That's the evidence you have before you from Mr. David Knechtel, who has known him for a number of years, Mr. Reid Schindel and Mr. James Ogston. They all knew him. 'Laid back, soft-spoken.' Their words, not mine. That's the evidence.

"What did the psychologist, Katherine Walz, tell you? Brian put her on a pedestal. A teddy bear-type. That's the evidence. It's not a situation where Brian has occasioned violence to Christine in the past, because Christine is not the type of woman who would accept that. And Brian is not the type of man to do something like that. That's the evidence.

"That's the evidence from Donna Henry, her best friend.

"That's the evidence from Cheryl MacMillan, a best friend.

"That's Brian Jack. That's the man we are dealing with."

I was perplexed by my adversary's constant endeavours to convince the jurors that Brian loved Christine very much and was dedicated to preserving their marriage. These things had never been questioned by Crown lawyers.

He persisted.

"We know that he tried everything within his power to keep that marriage together. He called Aunt Lidijia, who said she was from the old school, one who believes that when you married, you stayed married. Brian sought her help.

"He even wrote to Mr. Reiter, Christine's father. 'I'm looking for your help, Steve,' he wrote. Didn't get a reply. He wrote that letter, I think, in November, late November. 'My love for Christine can overcome all obstacles.'

"That's the evidence.

"To keep the marriage together, he sought out marriage counselling, saw a priest, told Peter Henry on the evening they played squash together at the Carlton Club that he wanted his marriage to remain intact. He had a commitment to the children, to Christine, to his faith. That's Brian Jack.

"But the most important piece of evidence which completes the picture did not come from Brian's mouth, and did not come from a best friend, where you could allege some kind of bias. The most important piece of evidence about him came from Christine's best friend. 'Like a sister,' Cheryl said. 'We were like sisters. Brian was soft-spoken, very generous, had lots of friends,' she said.

"But we know that," said counsel assuredly, as if he were expressing some universal truth. "We know that because that's the picture of Brian Jack as we go through witness after witness after witness who knew him. But most importantly, he was not a cold, calculating person!"

Abruptly, the studied voice of righteous indignation soared again.

"No, not a cold, calculating person, because the person that Crown counsel was talking about in his fanciful world of speculation was cold, calculating, diabolical. Not Brian Jack. Not according to the evidence. And I don't have to engage in any kind of guesswork because that's the hard evidence in this case.

"We know from the evidence that Brian Jack is the kind of person who would get things off his chest. He wore his emotions on his sleeve. He would even talk to people with whom he didn't have a current relationship with; he'd talk to them about his difficulties.

"For instance, he told Annette Clay that he pinned Chris down one time and he did that out of frustration, so that she would listen to him, about wanting to keep the marriage together. It wasn't an assault; it was so that Chris would listen to him. And he told that to Paulishyn and Schinkel, the Winnipeg Police who came to see him on December 22.

"Would a man who is a diabolical person, as the Crown would have you believe—the crafty Mr. Jack, I think he referred to him as—would that man tell the police and attract all kinds of attention to himself when he said to Paulishyn and Schinkel, 'I pinned her down once'? Why would he say that?

"Because he is being honest. His emotions are on his sleeve. He tells people if something has happened. Doesn't conceal it.

"You see, a guilty person wouldn't have done that. He wouldn't have drawn attention to himself. He wouldn't show a negative side of himself to the police of all people. Paulishyn and Schinkel? No! Why would he tell the police, Paulishyn and Schinkel, that he thought that Christine was afraid of him? That would conjure up all kinds of thoughts.

"Would a crafty, diabolical person do that? Or would a man, not cold, not calculating, who is honest and forthright, and who wears his emotions on his sleeve? That's the kind of man who would say that to the police. Because he had nothing to hide. Nothing to hide. He was not the man that Crown counsel, in all his eloquence, tried to make him out to be. That's not the evidence."

Richard Wolson, a staunch adherent to the maxim, "Repetition is the mother of learning," once again refreshed the jurors' memories.

"That's the kind of man Brian Jack is," he reminded them with gusto. "I'm not engaging in speculation when I say that. That's the evidence."

I guess we've all played armchair quarterback at one time or another. That's what I'm doing right now as I listen to a replay of the killer's counsel's closing address to the jury.

I think Richard Wolson made one terrible tactical error when he said:

"Even the so-called anonymous phone call which I'm going to deal with at some length at a later time..."

So-called? So-called? We proved beyond a reasonable doubt that Jack made the phone call. Here Wolson demonstrated a certain degree of desperation; he should have, quite frankly, left the matter of the phone call alone.

His recitation went on and on.

"Brian was in the police station with Officers Paulishyn and Schinkel. They asked him some questions and he denied making the phone call. Within a minute or two, but not as a result of cross-examination by Paulishyn and Schinkel, he said, 'Yes, I did, I made the phone call.'

"That's Brian Jack. He tells people if he's done something. That's Brian Jack. Not a diabolical, crafty person; not a cold, calculating person. That's the evidence."

I don't think this was a very carefully considered play. In fact, I'm inclined to think that it cost the Defence several yards.

❖ ❖ ❖ ❖ ❖

Good old solid, reliable, honest, what-you-see-is-what-you-get, teddy bear-type Brian Jack. That's the picture his counsel strove so hard to paint. Constant as the morning star.

It was Christine who had changed so dramatically. And Richard Wolson could handily point to the evidence to prove it.

He acknowledged that all the witnesses had said that she was generally a bubbly, upbeat, happy, outgoing person. But by the end of November and the beginning of December of 1988, she was going through a very difficult time. He then encapsulated the essence of the testimony of Cheryl MacMillan, Donna Mae Henry and Alfred Kircher, Christine's psycholgist, as it impacted on her physical and mental health.

"You don't have to be a psychologist or psychiatrist to understand that evidence," he stressed.

Laboriously, he then listed the symptoms: weight loss, sleeplessness, frequent crying spells and very little appetite.

He spoke of stress, emotional, financial and marital.

He mentioned the mood swings and the inner turmoil.

He alluded to a worsening situation as time progressed, feelings of guilt, indecisiveness, deficient motor response and lethargy.

He referred to Christine's atypical aloofness when her friends, the Henrys, came for dinner in December.

He again harkened back to the testimony of Alfred Kircher, who had cited feelings of helplessness and thoughts of suicide as additional symptoms of depression.

"There is no evidence that she was suicidal or plagued with feelings of helplessness," counsel conceded. "But all the other evidence is there;" he said authoritatively, "Christine Jack was someone who was depressed, someone who wasn't acting like herself."

Pausing then, as any great thespian might to ensure his audience's rapt attention, he spoke solemnly. "That's why she left on December seventeenth and that's why she was away for some time.

"She was seen December 23—that's hard, cold evidence—at the Charter House in the City of Winnipeg.

"You can explain or understand why she left. She wasn't herself."

❖ ❖ ❖ ❖ ❖

You can explain or understand something else, too: the inherent wisdom in that time-honoured aspiration of the masses, "The first thing we do, let's kill all the lawyers."[10]

It's outrageous. They are playing with a man's life.
—Richard Wolson

The Realm of Speculation

Had the producers of "The Young and the Restless" been hunting for a scriptwriter to add a new dimension to that television shows' love triangles, Richard Wolson was their man.

His rendition of Christine and Earl's dalliance in Grand Forks would have mesmerized any soap opera junkie, as would the rendezvous at Chi-Chi's Restaurant, the kissing, the hugging, the hand holding, the spark.

He gave his audience a glimpse of Christine's other world.

"But we know from Cheryl," he confided, "that these weren't ordinary times for Chris. Chris, Cheryl said, had 'the perfect storybook life, married to a football player, herself athletic in her endeavours, happy, nice house, nice things, good job. Then her world started to crumble around her.'"

The malleable voice of Richard Wolson was abruptly adjusted. Changing from the saccharine tones of the ham in a true romance to the raw rhetoric of the courtroom, he growled:

"Did Christine Jack and Earl Weber have a relationship? I know one thing. Everything seemed to change from the time she returned from Grand Forks. Her feelings toward Brian changed. At least that's what she told him. Everything seemed to change in their relationship from that time on.

"Did Christine leave December 17, 1988, in contemplation of furthering the relationship with Earl Weber?" Then, almost as an afterthought, Wolson added, "That's what Reid Schindel thought. 'It sure sounds suspicious to me,' Reid reckoned."

Clearly, the jurors weren't quite of the same mind as Brian Jack's pal, Reid Schindel.

The Realm of Speculation

❖ ❖ ❖ ❖ ❖

The next hurdle counsel had to jump concerned the wide disparities in the accused's account of the row he had had with Christine. So, too, the discrepancies in the times he told their friends that she had left. Wolson continued, "Now, my friend can stand up here and say to you as much as he likes, 'One time he said an argument, one time a heated argument, one time a shouting match, one time a discussion!' It's all the same thing. I would be suspicious. I would think you would be suspicious if Brian Jack talked to ten different people and told them all the exact pat story, word for word. You would think then, that, he had thought up a plan, that he had concocted a plan.

"It's all the same thing. They had an argument. There is no doubt about that. As to the words 'heated,' 'shouting match,' that's of no consequence. None whatsoever. An argument and Christine left.

"And then my friend the Crown attorney puts Brian under a microscope and he says to you, 'Examine the times. Examine the times. He told one person nine o'clock and someone else 9:15 or 9:30 and another between 9:00 and 10:00.'

"You wouldn't take a man's future from him based on that, between 9:00 and 10:00 would you?

"And if Brian Jack were lying, as intelligent as he is, don't you think that he could concoct a story and be consistent as to what time she left?

"Look what was happening to him when he called these people. Christine, his rock, his strength, had left. Do you think he was looking at the VCR like Peter Henry, 'Oh, it's now 9:27,' and noting the time? Do you think he would do that, I say facetiously? He was distraught, upset. If he were concocting a story, the times would be right, the words would be right, if he were the crafty Mr. Jack my friend tries to make him out to be. Be wary of someone who tells the same story all the time, ten times over, exactly the same, especially in these emotional circumstances, when he was crying and frantic."

Again the pregnant pause before yet another utterance.

"The words are of no great importance. The times are of no great importance. Christine left."

❖ ❖ ❖ ❖ ❖

Brian Jack did what he could to obliterate all traces of his wife's blood embedded in the couch cushion.

His counsel did what he could to obliterate it from the minds of the jurors.

The stratagem was simply to dwell on the myth of the spilled coffee and to ignore the blood stains. At the same time, taking a couple of swipes at Crown counsel couldn't hurt.

This segment of Richard Wolson's closing address to the jury qualified him for a gold medal in the windmill-tilting Olympics. He said:

"And Brian said to one of his friends, David MacMillan—and the Crown asked you to make a big to-do about it—he said that he spilled coffee. Do you think Brian Jack would mention that if it didn't happen? Because it would draw attention to him, that's what it would do. It would only draw attention, unless it happened, as Brian said it did.

"And, you know, sometimes when you go through a traumatic event—it's happened to all of us—your experience in life will tell you that, you think of the most innocuous, silly things. They just pop into your head like the fact that he spilled coffee.

They have no bearing on anything. Bringing up these things is a smoke screen put up by the Crown, nothing more, to argue that before you. He wouldn't be doing something to draw attention to himself if he was that crafty, diabolical person that Mr. Montgomery would have you believe. That's totally and absolutely inconsistent with the evidence in this case.

"But he told the police that he sat around, he did some housework. Isn't it interesting that Cheryl MacMillan, when she was awakened by the call, that's what she did to pass the time? She told you, 'I did some housework, some things I wouldn't ordinarily do.'

"Perhaps it was cleaning the stove or some things we don't like to do ordinarily, just to pass the time. That's what Brian did while waiting for Chris to come back."

"A big to-do."

A "to-do" is defined in the *Random House Dictionary of the English Language* as bustle, fuss, making much ado about trifles.

The ladies and gentlemen of this jury were not inclined to equate spilled blood with trifles.

By definition, a "smoke screen" is something intended to disguise, conceal or deceive; to camouflage.

Attempting to deceive jurors has never appealed to me.

❖ ❖ ❖ ❖ ❖

The Realm of Speculation

Brian Jack was insistent. He had knocked on the Henrys' door around 3:00 o'clock that Sunday morning.

Peter Henry was equally adamant. He hadn't.

Another imbroglio facing the hard-pressed Richard Wolson.

I recalled with gleeful satisfaction a former Chief Justice cautioning a lawyer to "cut out the fancy footwork."

This admonition came to mind when Richard donned his dancing slippers, pirouetted in front of the jury box and cried out:

"And then he told you, told the police, he told Mr. Knechtel, 'I fell asleep, and woke up at 3:00 or 3:30.'

"Now, if you woke up at 3:30—and you remember time wasn't important to him, particularly under the emotions of the situation—he wasn't looking at his VCR or clock in the house, noting the time. Time wasn't important to Brian at the best of times, let alone in the emotional upheaval of that evening. If he woke up as he told Dave Knechtel—and why would he tell him this if it weren't true—at 3:30, he would get up shortly thereafter, as he said. Then he went to the Henrys' residence and knocked on the door. They didn't answer and he went back home. That would be sometime after 3:30.

"Those aren't the words of a lawyer talking to you, that's the evidence.

"He said to the police that he went to the Henrys' at approximately three o'clock. What does that mean? He told Mr. Knechtel that he woke up at 3:00 or 3:30, and he went to the Henrys'. That's all consistent. It's all consistent.

"If you want to look at time, if you want to analyze time, for instance, Peter Henry said, 'I stopped watching the VCR at 3:29.' And then he has this ritual, he said, before he'd get to bed at about 3:45.

"But what did Donna say? Donna said Peter came to bed at 3:30. That's what Donna told you. Time doesn't mean that much. You're not going to take a man's future for 15 minutes or half an hour in the circumstances of this case.

"Why would he even tell the police, if it weren't true, that he went to Peter Henry's? What would be the motive in that? Why? It's of no relevance. But he told them because that's what he did. He told people because it was true.

"There is no other reason to say that he went to Peter Henry's house. Why would he tell the police this unless it were true, as he told Dave Knechtel, that he woke up at about 3:30, and shortly thereafter he went to the Henrys', knocked on the door, got no answer, and came back home. And when he came back home, Adam and Kairsten were up. He cuddled with them and put them back to bed. That's the Brian Jack we know, the devoted father, the one who cares."

More than one quizzical eyebrow was raised in the jury box as Richard dug in his heels.

"Do you think he would leave his children at home all night while he was driving out in the country, as my friend would have you believe, with Christine in the back, having killed her? That doesn't make any sense. That's not Brian Jack. That's a dream of the Crown, a conjecture, a supposition, a guess.

"Brian was home that night, except for the time that he went to the Henrys', probably shortly after he woke up, which he told Knechtel was about 3:00 or 3:30. He was home. That's what he told the police. And he told the police that for one reason and one reason only, and that's because it's true. He was home."

I got the feeling during Richard's lengthy soft-shoe routine that he had put his foot in his mouth more than once.

❖ ❖ ❖ ❖ ❖

Richard, like the wind, could rapidly change direction.

"This leads us to Ste. Anne," he stormed. "You see, I'm not going to do what the Crown did in his speech to you yesterday. I'm not going to gloss over certain points which stand out and must be talked about.

"You remember how he glossed over the evidence of Shirley Garbutt and Donna Pike? And I was surprised as he just glossed over it. What did he say? Oh, honest people but not concerned. And that was it. Four and a half hours he talked to you yesterday. And that was it.

"And you know why that was it? Because it's irrefutable, hard, cold evidence: Christine Jack was at the Charter House on December 23. This was the evidence of Shirley Garbutt and Donna Pike."

At this point, Wolson requested, and was happily granted, a brief recess. When the Court reconvened 20 minutes later, Wolson resumed in high gear. The next half-hour was consumed with his analysis of the testimony of the witnesses from Ste. Anne.

"I'm not going to do what the Crown has done and gloss over the evidence that's important. It must be dealt with. I'd like to look with you at the evidence of the witnesses from Ste. Anne," he said. "And I'd like you to put their evidence under a microscope."

I tarry at this point, just long enough to wonder whether Richard has some kind of a fetish about microscopes.

"Brian Jack has nothing to prove," he insisted. "He is presumed innocent. Don't put him under a microscope. Put these witnesses under a microscope. Look at their evidence very carefully."

Counsel stressed the unreliability of the Ste. Anne witnesses. Essentially, he contended, their testimony was flawed by dint of too many obvious discrepancies.

The reliability of the testimony of the women from the Charter House, by contrast, was unassailable.

"Look at their evidence carefully," Richard admonished the jurors.

Thankfully, they did.

❖ ❖ ❖ ❖ ❖

During the dynamic Defence counsel's two-and-a-half hour address, he reserved some of his more vitriolic prose for the lawmen.

"Now, I have referred earlier to the police investigation, this non-investigation," he said irritably. "Inadequate, grossly negligent and, without question, one-sided. Bent on one thing only. Not the truth of the matter, bent on one avenue only, to point to Mr. Jack, to take every fact in the case and reconcile it, not with his innocence, as the law says, but with his guilt."

At the height of this cop-bashing, he again lashed out:

"The very day Brian Jack is at the police station, on December 24, a call came in that a person saw Christine Jack in the Blazer driving down St. Mary's Road on December 22. It's outrageous. Never checked.

"You're going to take a man's future from him, the Crown asks you, on that kind of evidence? What a travesty. At trials where people have been found guilty, and later proven innocent, there haven't been these kinds of obvious errors.

And why didn't Paulishyn and Schinkel check these things out? And isn't this a pretty sad, sad state of affairs?

"'Mr. Wolson,' Schinkel said to me, 'we didn't check them out because we thought Mr. Jack was involved in what happened on December 17, so we didn't check them out.'

"He thought. Judge, jury, jailer, that's what he thought. Can you imagine? Somebody—can you imagine? Somebody says they saw the woman and they don't check it out? Are we living in a police state?

"Do you take a man's future from him based on that? That one man formed an opinion and, therefore, put blinkers on and didn't check out matters that were of grave importance, matters that could free that man, Mr. Jack? No, because that wasn't the intent of these officers."

Trials & Errors: The People vs. Brian Gordon Jack

❖   ❖   ❖   ❖   ❖

My first words to the ladies and gentlemen of this jury at the commencement of the trial on Monday, September 10, 1990, were simply:

> It is the position of the Crown that Christine Anna Jack is dead and that Brian Gordon Jack is responsible for her death; that he had the opportunity to kill her and a motive for so doing.

At no time did I speak of the Crown's theory. It didn't have one.

I told the jurors that I was sure that His Lordship would instruct them that they were entitled to draw logical inferences from proven facts.

I am neither a registered soothsayer nor am I endowed with the gift of prophecy. It's just that history, like Richard Wolson, repeats itself. I had heard his harangue on the theory of the Crown on prior occasions. We could have delivered it in unison.

"I would like to review with you the Crown's theory," he said. "When I say 'theory,' what the Crown did, what Mr. Montgomery did, was he entered into the realm of speculation."

Counsel then embarked upon an exhaustive review of my comments.

At one point he scoffed:

"It's outrageous. It just doesn't pass the test of common sense. And that's the theory. That's the speculation that my friend wants you to accept."

Richard likes the word "outrageous." He uses it a lot.

The deeper he delved into Crown counsel's discourse, the more agitated he became. "Examine that?" he demanded. "Put it under a microscope. Don't put Brian Jack under a microscope. Putting him under a microscope doesn't pass the test of common sense."

Another one of Richard's favourite words is "ridiculous." He uses it a lot, too. "And then you think that Brian Jack is the kind of person that would go home and start phoning people and fabricate this story? And fabricate it in such a way that he didn't have the times down right and didn't have the elements of the story down right? That's ridiculous. Ridiculous. An imbecile wouldn't do that, let alone a man who has the education of Mr. Jack.

"It's a ridiculous theory. And that's what happens with theories. You can say anything. It's just a theory. Try and impress you with that nonsense? It's outrageous, especially in the backdrop of this non-investigation."

Richard, normally subdued, a man of quiet dignity outside the courtroom, was working up quite a lather.

I don't know if she is going to come back and if she does, I don't know how she will feel about me.

"Why would Brian Jack say that? Doesn't make any sense if he killed her. And it doesn't pass the test of common sense. And that's what jurors use, common sense, every day, plain common sense.

"And it doesn't make any sense for only one reason, because Brian Jack is not guilty. Brian Jack didn't do that. The theory doesn't deserve a second look or a second thought."

Unexpectedly, the strident voice of the screech owl gave way to the murmuring sound of the dove.

Richard spoke softly.

"I can't tell you where Christine Jack is. I wish I could. But I know, and you know, that on December 22 and December the 23 she was seen. More specifically, on December 23 at the Charter House Hotel between five and six o'clock, she was seen.

"I don't know where she is. I don't know if some ill fate has befallen her. But I know that on December 23 she was at the Charter House. And I know that Brian Jack did not commit the murder of his rock, of his strength, of his reason for being."

❖ ❖ ❖ ❖ ❖

The killer's able counsel was moving into the home stretch with a final reminder that Shirley Garbutt and Donna Pike had seen Christine Jack six days after she had allegedly been murdered. The waitresses had seen her and that's all there was to it.

It was outrageous that Brian Jack should have been put on trial for this alleged murder when it was obvious that Christine was alive. Outrageous!

Like his mentor, Clarence Darrow, Richard Wolson was not at all reluctant to direct his ire against any number of individuals. "Beanie" Kaplan was another victim whom he had singled out for examination.

"And my friend, the crafty Mr. Kaplan, had the audacity, when he was cross-examining these two witnesses, to suggest that they had done something wrong in that they didn't keep calling the police department. Can you imagine that?

"These two women phoned the police department. Mrs. Pike leaves a number where she's at in Brandon and gives the information. And my friend has the audacity to suggest that you shouldn't listen to Mrs. Pike or Mrs. Garbutt because they didn't keep calling back, when my friend knew the very essence of that evidence which I never got it until September of '89? It's outrageous, absolutely outrageous.

"It's outrageous to take Brian Jack's life and play with it like that.

"Now, Cheryl MacMillan said that Christine's hair was streaked. Mrs. Pike wouldn't have known that when she gave her description to the police. It just confirms—not that confirmation is needed—it just confirms the evidence that Christine Jack was in the Charter House on December 23. And that's undeniable evidence, unshaken, because it's true."

The stern voice of the defender abated. A funereal tone befit the final word.

"I can't tell you, and I wish I could," counsel said with great solemnity, "where Christine Jack is today. I wish I could. But I know that on December 23, Christine Jack was alive.

"In closing, I suggest to you that the Crown must prove its case beyond a reasonable doubt. It has not. I stand before you now and I ask you to bring back the only verdict that you can in this case: not guilty.

"Brian Jack begs you for the only verdict that you can give in this case: not guilty.

"The evidence in this case cries out for that one verdict: not guilty.

"Thank you."

It is tempting to say that after such a lengthy charge, it did not matter much what the judge told the jury, but such a cynical comment would do an injustice to the jury's oath.
—Chief Justice Richard Scott

The Longest Day

Benjamin Hewak is not a loquacious man. Even while telling a joke, ribald or otherwise, he effectively sets the stage for the punch line with a paucity of words.

It is almost inconceivable then that on November 15, 1990, he talked to this jury for more than 11 hours.

Seldom does a judge's charge in a murder trial exceed an hour or two. What was there about this case, one might wonder, which icompelled the Chief Justice to exceed the norm five times over?

Perhaps there is a simple explanation. An exceedingly verbose Crown attorney addressed the jury for well in excess of four hours the preceding Monday. A rather voluble Defence counsel presented his argument the following day. He was on his feet for over two and a half hours.

The Chief, wise to the wiles and whining of courtroom lawyers, shrewdly revisited the territory covered by both counsels. This took a long, long time. Nevertheless, it circumvented criticism for having failed to fully advance the position of the Crown or to present a fair replication of the Defence.

There is, however, much more to a judge's charge in a criminal trial than a mere allusion to, or rehash of, the case for the Crown and a repetition of the stance taken by the prisoner.

The summing-up of the facts and the law in a criminal case is rightly considered to be a very important part of the trial of the accused. It is universally accepted that a summing-up should outline the law, review the evidence, define the issues and instruct the jury as to all matters necessary to enable them to fairly consider the issues in the case before them.

Chief Justice Hewak did all of these things.

Sir James F. Stephen, an eminent English jurist and historian, wrote:

> I think that a judge who merely states to the jury certain propositions of law and then reads over his notes does not discharge his duty. I also think that a judge who forms a decided opinion before he hears the whole case, or who allows himself to be, in any degree, actuated by an advocate's feelings, in regulating the proceedings, all together fails to discharge his duty; but I further think that he ought not to conceal his opinion from the jury, nor do I see how it is possible for him to do so, if he arranges the evidence in the order in which it strikes his mind. The mere effort to see what is essential to a story, in what order the important events happened, and in what relation they stand to each other, must of necessity point to some conclusion. The act of stating for the jury the question which they have to answer and of stating the evidence bearing on these questions and showing in what respects it is important, generally goes a considerable way towards suggesting an answer to them; and, if a judge does not do as much at least as this, he does almost nothing.[11]

The Brian Jack trial spanned ten weeks. To compress its essence into a meaningful segment of the charge to the jury was a formidable task. Chief Justice Hewak did it well.

Lord Chief Justice Goddard, of the English Court of Criminal Appeal, said:

> I have often wondered whether any criminal case lasting over two or three hours has ever yet been tried by a judge, even a judge most experienced in criminal matters, in which it was not possible to come before this Court and raise some question of misdirection.[12]

As this case lingered on for the better part of three months, it was inevitable that Tiger Wolson would go before the Court of Appeal and raise questions of misdirection. He would contend that the trial judge had erred in law 23 times during the course of his charge.

The Longest Day

Chief Justice Scott said of the Hewak summing-up:

> The length of the charge itself was a separate ground of appeal. The charge, while not perfect (and what charge is?), in the end adequately put all the issues but one fairly before the jury.[13]

Courtroom lawyers are a fickle lot. Had the charge been of two hours' duration rather than 11, you could have safely bet your last buck that its brevity would have been assailed and listed among the grounds of appeal.

Sir James Stephen joined the great majority more than a hundred years ago—1894 to be precise. I deeply regret that circumstances preclude my furnishing Sir James with a photocopy of the charge in the Jack case, for his evaluation.

Had I been able to arrange this assessment, there is no doubt in my mind that the venerable jurist would have said, "There was nothing wrong with that summing-up. Young Ben did a damn good job of it."

❖ ❖ ❖ ❖ ❖

Eleven weary jurors, then sequestered, were escorted from the courthouse to their hotel at 11:15 p.m.

They would begin their deliberations the following morning at ten o'clock sharp.

I just met with Brian. He's somewhat downtrodden, very disappointed with the verdict. But he has confidence that somewhere down the line he will be vindicated.
—Richard Wolson

The Verdict

Guilty!

Two men and nine women deliberated for just four and a half hours before returning to the courtroom. They were unanimous. Brian Jack was guilty of murder in the second degree.

He was immediately sentenced to imprisonment for life. Further, he would have to serve ten years before he would be eligible to apply for parole.

❖   ❖   ❖   ❖   ❖

As an old stager, I knew only too well that this was not the final curtain. It was just the end of the first act.

Richard moved quickly to set the stage for the next performance. Within four days of the conviction, he had filed a Notice of Appeal. It affirmed that the verdict was perverse and that a new trial should be granted.

He was most anxious to have Jack admitted to bail pending the outcome of the appeal. There was little likelihood of it being heard for at least a year.

Nine days after the conviction, he appeared before Mr. Justice Philp, hell-bent on securing his client's release. After all, he stressed, Jack had been out on bail before his trial and hadn't caused any problems.

His Lordship was clearly unimpressed.

"This was the ultimate crime of domestic violence," he said, "and a reasonable, right-thinking person might lose confidence and respect for the judicial system if he were released."

Then, almost as an afterthought, he said: "The accused comes to this court as a convicted criminal. He is no longer clothed with the presumption of innocence."

Bail was denied.

There have been times when I have applauded Richard Wolson's perseverance on behalf of a client.

There have been times, too, when his obstinacy has irritated me.

Still, if I were in the prisoner's dock, his eternal persistence would have given me reason to hope.

Precisely three weeks after his overture before Mr. Justice Philp, the tenacious Wolson stood before a three-man panel in the Court of Appeal.

His mission—to have the Philp decision overturned—was doomed from the start.

Chief Justice Scott, speaking for a unanimous court, put it succinctly. "Only in exceptional circumstances," he said, "will a convicted murderer be released on bail."

Judges are apt to be naïve, simple-minded men.
—Justice Oliver Wendell Holmes

Reversal

They ordered a new trial for Brian Gordon Jack, did Chief Justice Scott, Mr. Justice O'Sullivan and Mr. Justice Philp.

I read the judgment. It disturbed me. There was a time when the words of Daniel, "Thou art weighed in the balances and art found wanting," when applied to the Justices, would have assuaged my distress.

But that was yesterday.

This judgment, in my opinion, put another gigantic crack in our, to borrow from Chief Justice Lamer's delicate phraseology, "already fragile justice system."

Before turning to the decision and losing the reader in a labyrinth of legalistic illogic, a line or two about each member of the panel might prove insightful.

One of the scribes at Winnipeg's oldest daily newspaper, the *Winnipeg Free Press*, prepared these thumbnail sketches:

Richard Scott

The Chief Justice, appointed in August 1990, is universally liked and respected. "He's as close as you can get to a perfect judge," says one lawyer.

The former associate chief justice of Court of Queen's Bench was appointed to the bench in 1985, after a distinguished 22-year career as a civil litigator.

Scott wins praise from lawyers for his even-handed demeanour and his courtesy. A gentleman is the way most describe Scott, a former Law Society of Manitoba president.

Though he's undoubtedly a tory, judge-watchers peg him as a moderate.

Joseph O'Sullivan

Aggressive, cantankerous and controversial is the way most lawyers describe the senior member of the Court, who went directly to the bench in 1975.

The winner of the gold medal in law at the University of Manitoba in 1953, O'Sullivan is well known for his legal scholarship—apparently a double-edged sword he wields freely when hearing cases.

"His brilliance is his biggest problem," notes one lawyer. "He uses his mind to ridicule counsel."

Tales of stormy appearances before the frail-looking O'Sullivan, who often appears ill-prepared, are legendary.

A staunch Roman Catholic and life-long bachelor with a quick temper, he has a reputation for shooting from the lip.

The former civil litigator is seen as having liberal leanings in his judgments, being Defence-oriented and generally supporting the Charter of Rights and Freedoms.

Allan Philp

Philp has worked his way up through the judicial ranks, having started as Chief of the County Court in 1973 and then being elevated to the highest court in 1983.

He is seen as an effective team player on the court who writes careful decisions. As for his ideological leanings, he's hard to read. While tough on sentencing, he is generally regarded as a middle-of-the-road justice who often holds the swing vote on the Court's panels.[14]

❖ ❖ ❖ ❖ ❖

In what can only be characterized as one colossal understatement, Chief Justice Scott wrote:

> It is a pity to have to send a matter of this complexity back for a new trial because of an isolated error in an otherwise acceptable charge.

The greater pity, in my judgment, is that a grievous error was committed not by Chief Justice Hewak, but by Chief Justice Scott and the panel over which he presided. Had they but harkened to the maxim, "Let the judges answer to the question of law and the jurors to the matter of fact," Brian Jack would have been carted off to prison and public confidence in the justice system would have been partially restored.

❖ ❖ ❖ ❖ ❖

Chief Justice Hewak had commenced his instructions to the jury at 10 a.m. on November 15 and concluded at 9:30 p.m. the same day. As a result of certain matters counsel raised for clarification purposes, a recharge didn't terminate until 11:02 p.m.

This was a very long charge, totaling in all, inclusive of breaks for lunch and dinner, more than 11 hours.

The length of the judge's charge was itself, ironically, one of the Appellant's 23 grounds of appeal. An intolerant Thomas Jefferson on one occasion was heard to shout: "For God's sake, let us freely hear both sides!"

Surely this admonition was in the back of the trial judge's mind as he laboriously revisited the case presented by both the Crown and the Defence.

❖ ❖ ❖ ❖ ❖

I have always been mildly amused by the manner in which some appeal court justices try to let off easily errant judges in the lower courts.

The lofty prelude, "While I do not wish to be unduly critical of the judge in the court below," usually precedes a swift, verbal kick in the ass.

Chief Justice Scott, in alluding to the testimony of Shirley Garbutt and Donna Pike, the witnesses from the Charter House, wrote:

> As will be noted in more detail later, both witnesses gave their evidence in a very forceful manner and displayed no evident signs of weakness in memory.

While I do not wish to be unduly critical of the Chief Justice's appraisal of the manner in which Garbutt and Pike testified, his assessment, putting it most charitably, was way off the rails. Their delivery was far from forceful; their memories were not like steel traps.

His Lordship's view of the witnesses was from the lifeless pages of transcript of their testimony.

I saw and heard them speak. The witness box was less than two car lengths away from the Crown counsel table.

❖ ❖ ❖ ❖ ❖

The Notice of Appeal advanced 23 separate and distinct grounds.

It was the contention of the killer's counsel that each and every one of them set forth an error of sufficient gravity to warrant a new trial.

He mounted a relentless attack on the judge's charge and recharge. His Lordship's mistakes, he argued, if not individually then collectively, resulted in errors of such cumulative effect as to call for a reversal.

The appellate justices found 22 of the 23 grounds devoid of merit.

The appellant found fault with the comparisons that the trial judge made between the Ste. Anne and Charter House witnesses. The judges of the Court of Appeal saw merit in this criticism.

It was this one issue, this "isolated error in an otherwise acceptable charge," that necessitated a new trial.

After having mulled over the Scott Court judgment at least four times, the words of Lord Mansfield struck in me a most responsive chord:

> Give your decisions, never your reasons; your decisions may be right, your reasons are sure to be wrong.

Chief Justice Scott struck the passing bell. The pronouncement of the prosecution's doom was inherent in his reasons.

He wrote:

> The trial judge summarized the evidence of the various witnesses (and in the course of so doing, related such testimony to the issues) in a chronological order. He therefore dealt with the evidence of the Ste. Anne witnesses before that of the Charter House witnesses. With respect to the former, he provided an appropriate and strong warning about the danger of eyewitness-identification evidence in general, and their evidence in particular. He noted the many inconsistencies in the specifics of the identification of the 'stranger' who had arrived in Ste. Anne on the evening of December 17, 1988 with a disabled vehicle.

He said:

> Before you accept it, you should look for other evidence that would support your conclusion that the identification of the man as Brian Jack is accurate, even though there may be inconsistencies between the evidence of the various eyewitnesses who testified.

When almost at the very end of the summary of the witnesses' evidence, and indeed of the charge itself, he returned to the issue of identification evidence when reviewing the testimony of Garbutt and Pike. He again sounded a warning about being 'extremely careful' in considering the evidence of eyewitnesses, particularly when identifying strangers. He then analyzed, as he had with the Ste. Anne witnesses, some similarities and differences in their evidence. He went on to say:

> So, you can see that there is a need for you to be extremely careful when you consider this evidence of eyewitness identification. Before you accept it, you should look for other evidence that might support your conclusion that the identification of the woman as Christine Jack is accurate, even though there may be inconsistencies within the evidence of the various eyewitnesses who testified.

The trial judge immediately thereafter noted that, whereas with respect to the Ste. Anne witnesses there was other evidence independent of their identification of the man, such as identification of the Blazer by Hudrick and St. Marie, which could help decide if, in fact, they had correctly identified Brian Jack;

> Here, with these witnesses (Pike and Garbutt), you do not have such independent evidence. You have, basically, identification by two witnesses who primarily relied on the face and hair of the woman. As I've said, you should be extremely careful when you consider this evidence.

Finally, he reviewed the evidence of the Charter House witnesses fairly, and in considerable detail. Immediately after giving his instructions with respect to these witnesses, he reminded the jury one last time of the presumption of innocence and the necessity for the Crown to prove its case beyond a reasonable doubt.

Counsel for the accused takes strong exception to the way in which the charge 'juxtaposed' the evidence of the Ste. Anne and Charter House witnesses and, in the process, appeared to apply the same test to witnesses called by the Crown as to those called by the Court.

It was not necessary that there be independent evidence in order for the testimony of Pike and Garbutt to raise a reasonable doubt. Nor was the evidence of the Ste. Anne witnesses and the Charter House witnesses counterposed in that the jury, so it is argued, could have accepted the evidence of both groups of witnesses and still have acquitted the accused. This latter submission may be theoretically possible, but it is difficult to see how the jury, if they did conclude that the Crown had established beyond a reasonable doubt that Brian Jack had traveled to Ste. Anne in the Blazer on the evening of December 17, 1988 (with all that such a conclusion entails, including the inherent fabrication and deception), could have at the same time accepted the evidence of the Charter House witnesses. But this is not the principal area of concern.

The critical issue in this case is whether the trial judge unfairly disparaged the evidence of the Charter House witnesses by inferring that there was a burden of proof with respect to 'acceptance' of their evidence upon the accused. The warning and caution given with respect to the Ste. Anne witnesses was necessary and apt. They were witnesses called by the Crown in support of a case based almost entirely on circumstantial evidence. Pike and Garbutt, on the other hand, were called by the Court (in reality to assist the Defence). If their evidence caused the jury to have a reasonable doubt as to whether Christine Jack was alive on December 23, 1988, then the accused was entitled to be acquitted. This the trial judge failed entirely to deal with.

The initial caution about the eyewitness identification of the Charter House witnesses was not inappropriate in the context of the charge as a whole. There was, however, a clear suggestion that the jury had to 'accept' the evidence of the Charter House witnesses presumably before drawing inferences from it favourable to the accused, but that, unlike the evidence of the Ste. Anne witnesses, there was no supporting independent evidence. This suggestion was wrong. In my opinion, a fair analogy can be made between identification witnesses in this case, particularly the Charter House witnesses, and alibi witnesses. Indeed, in a very real sense the evidence of Garbutt and Pike dealt with the same kind of 'time and place' testimony critical to a consideration of alibi evidence called on behalf of an accused. The law is clear that an alibi need not be proved; it need only raise a reasonable doubt in the minds of the jury.

In my opinion, the jury in this case ought to have been charged as follows:

> If the jury accepted the evidence of the Charter House witnesses, they were entitled to (and, indeed probably should) return a verdict of not guilty;
> Even if they did not accept the evidence of those two witnesses, but were left in a reasonable doubt by it, they should also return a

verdict of not guilty; and

Even if not left with a reasonable doubt by the evidence of Garbutt and Pike, they should still go on to determine whether or not on the basis of all of the evidence, the accused was guilty beyond a reasonable doubt.[15]

❖ ❖ ❖ ❖ ❖

Richard Saull, the erudite little bulldog who appeared for the Crown Respondent in the Court of Appeal, argued forcefully. His position could be put in a nutshell: the error, if there was one, in the context of all the other issues and the overwhelming evidence of guilt, was of a trifling nature.

Saull invited the appellate justices to apply the "no miscarriage of justice" proviso of the Criminal Code in the event that they concluded that there was an error in the charge with respect to the Charter House witnesses. As Chief Justice Scott declared,

> The problem for the Crown here, is that this evidence was of the utmost importance to the Defence since it was the only evidence which was capable of placing Christine Jack at some specific location (and alive) after the evidence of December 17, 1988.
>
> Far from being unimportant, because it came at the end of a long day and of a very lengthy charge, its location there was of singular importance to the Defence. It was, literally, the last word about the evidence before the members of the jury were invited to retire and consider their verdict.

❖ ❖ ❖ ❖ ❖

Judges across this country constantly affirm their confidence in the intelligence and ability of the modern jury. Oftentimes, however, their comments belie their professed trust.

I have never been able to comprehend the appellate judges' grave concern about the order in which the trial judge dealt with the evidence of the Charter House witnesses. The time of night when the Garbutt-Pike testimony was reviewed apparently distressed them.

Had Their Lordships placed any reliance whatsoever on the common sense and the competence of the jurors, the time this instruction was given would have been irrelevant. In fact, had they been charged on the implications of the Charter House evidence at 10:30 in the morning, or three o'clock in the afternoon, or 10:15 at night, their conclusion would have been the same—Christine Jack was not dining in the Rib Room of the Charter House on the evening of December 23, 1988.

❖ ❖ ❖ ❖ ❖

There has been a sorry history of cop-bashing on the part of some judges in this jurisdiction.

Defence counsel and the judges of the Scott panel voiced strong criticism of the police for belated or non-disclosure of alleged sightings of Christine Jack. Their fault-finding was intemperate and unfortunate.

The judgment was peppered with condemnatory phrases such as, "No matter how regrettable (or worse) the conduct of the police was..."

One particularly distasteful and unwarranted slight was manifested in a sentence which began, "The Charter is not a remedy for police abuse..."

I weary of the carping of those critics who sit in the relative security of their chambers, ignorant of or oblivious to all that is entailed in a major police investigation.

No, the police didn't "follow up" on every alleged sighting of Christine Jack. And for good reason.

It was during Richard Wolson's vigorous cross-examination of Detective Loren Schinkel, one of the major investigators in the case, that the following exchange took place:

> Wolson: And if you had been told that somebody saw Christine Jack, you wouldn't bother to go and speak to that person and check that out? You wouldn't bother doing that? Is that your evidence?
> Schinkel: No, because in my mind what had transpired in the family room at 170 Alburg Drive on the night of December 17 had led to her death and her husband was involved in that.

> *The beginning of the words of his mouth is foolishness; and the end of his talk is mischievous madness.*
> —Ecclesiastes 10:13

The O'Sullivan Concurrence

"I am in substantial agreement with the reasons of Chief Justice Scott," wrote Mr. Justice Joseph O'Sullivan,

> and, like him, I too would order a new trial. Since we are ordering a new trial, it would be usual to comment as little as possible on evidentiary matters but I agree this is an unusual case. I think Chief Justice Scott has fairly summarized the evidence and he is right when he says the picture that emerges from the evidence is that Mrs. Jack was a loving, caring mother who would not willingly abandon her children, family and friends whatever the personal provocation. I think that view was probably true.

Why O'Sullivan then saw fit to overstep the bounds of common decency defies reason. He continued:

> However, in my opinion another view is possible, and that is that Mrs. Jack was a two-timing, deceitful and scheming woman who was infatuated with her boyfriend and who might be quite prepared to abandon a husband she no longer had any feeling for, after making arrangements with a friend to look after her children in the event of her disappearance. She consulted a lawyer and may have been told that there was no way she could disentangle her life from his without walking out. I do not say this view is likely, but it is possible. It would be for a jury at the next trial to consider the various possibilities when they are deliberating what inferences

to draw from the evidence of the extraordinary events of December 1988."

❖   ❖   ❖   ❖   ❖

On January 3, 1992, Chief Justice Scott released the judgment of the Court of Appeal in *Regina v. Jack*. Unfortunately, the O'Sullivan segment was included.

Intellectually dishonest, morally reprehensible and mean-spirited, it managed, nonetheless, to pass muster before the Chief Justice and Mr. Justice Philp, as well.

To my dying day, I will never understand why these two highly respected jurists permitted themselves to become signatories to a judgment that included the injudicious comments of their colleague, O'Sullivan: "...a two-timing, deceitful and scheming woman who was infatuated with her boyfriend..."

From the pen of one sworn to uphold the law, a judge of the Court of Appeal no less, such callous, vacuous, refutable conjecture is unforgivable.

Make no mistake. What O'Sullivan irrationally implied was that it would be open to another jury to conclude that Christine Jack was a shameless, immoral woman, a veritable Jezebel.

I can only assume that he studied the transcripts of the trial evidence before writing his ill-conceived, unconscionable judgment.

"Two-timing"?

Where is the evidence that Christine Jack was unfaithful to her husband, Brian?

"Deceitful"?

Where is the evidence that she was duplicitous, fraudulent and given to trickery and double-dealing?

"Scheming"?

Where is the evidence of crafty plotting? Where is the evidence of sly and underhanded planning?

During ten weeks of trial, not a shred of evidence of scheming surfaced.

"Boyfriend"?

Christine Jack did not have a boyfriend.

This was not the first time I had turned to Holy Writ after having suffered the caustic comments of the cynical O'Sullivan. For there it is written, "The words of a wise man's mouth are gracious; but the lips of a fool will swallow up himself."[16]

O'Sullivan also wrote:

> I am concerned about the judge's charge that the jury should rely only on the evidence presented before it. I think the jury was entitled to draw inferences unfavourable to the Crown because of the failure to call witnesses.

And to borrow from the words of Dickens' Mr. Bumble, "If the law supposes that, the law is an ass—an idiot."[17]

His Lordship then stated:

> Drawing adverse inferences is not speculation. Defence counsel was entitled to ask (I do not say he did ask) where was the fingerprint evidence, if any; where were the DNA test results, if any; where were the witnesses who claimed to have seen Mrs. Jack after the alleged time of her death; where was the young son of Mr. Jack, the son who must have seen material incidents the night of the alleged disappearance?

As to these potential witnesses, the judge told the jury: "You may wish to have heard from them, but you cannot guess what they may have said."

In my opinion, the members of the jury were entitled to infer that what they would have said would be unfavourable to the Crown's case.

It is, and always has been, the prerogative of Crown counsel to select those persons whose testimony could advance the case for the Prosecution.

Chief Justice Scott himself acknowledged this self-evident truth when he referred to "the discretion which a Prosecutor undoubtedly still has to determine which witnesses to call."

Joseph Francis O'Sullivan, during his days at the bar, never prosecuted anyone, even for a crime as dastardly as a breach of the dog pound bylaw. And, yet, he recklessly alluded to the Crown's failure to call certain witnesses. An unduly paranoid prosecutor might infer that he was being chastised for his omission, or neglect, or even dereliction perhaps.

"Where was the fingerprint evidence, if any?" O'Sullivan suggested defence counsel was entitled to ask.

No doubt Brian Jack's fingerprints were left on the glass from which he quaffed the Old Vienna beer in the Ste. Anne pub on the night of

December 17, 1988. And no doubt the glass was washed several times before he became a suspect.

The chances of discovery of fingerprint evidence, implicating Brian Jack in the murder of his wife, were rather remote in this case—about as unlikely as finding his prints on the ceiling of the Sistine Chapel.

The learned appeal court justice knew full well that had there been fingerprint evidence implicating the accused, Mr. Wolson would have been so advised, either by police or by Crown counsel. He wouldn't have needed to ask.

Mr. Justice O'Sullivan said that Defence counsel was entitled to ask where the DNA test results were, if any.

Mr. Wolson didn't need to ask. He already knew. The testing had not been completed at the time the trial got under way.

While dealing with pre-trial delays, Chief Justice Scott observed that:

> The trial was originally set for May 7, 1990 but adjourned at the request of the Crown on May 2, 1990 to September 10, 1990. The request for an adjournment was made to enable the Crown to obtain DNA blood-typing evidence. Counsel for the accused strenuously objected to the adjournment for a number of reasons, including his contention that there had been unreasonable delay to the prejudice of Brian Jack. The trial judge concluded there had been neither unreasonable delay nor prejudice demonstrated in a further delay of some four months to enable the DNA testing to be completed. He therefore granted the adjournment.
>
> The DNA testing was not completed by September 1990, however, and the trial in fact proceeded without it.
>
> I am satisfied that even though the DNA blood-typing evidence was not in fact used or available, the adjournment was requested by the Crown in good faith and reasonably and appropriately granted. Had the DNA evidence in fact become available, it was hoped that it would establish with scientific certainty the identity of the person whose blood was found on the Blazer's tailgate and on the pillow stuffing from the family room of the Jack residence.

I first heard tell of DNA typing—at the time a leading edge technology—in the summer of 1989 during the Brian Jack preliminary inquiry. However, the wonders of molecular genetics were as foreign to me as Einstein's theory of relativity.

Phil Hodge, the enterprising young serologist from the local Crime

Detection Laboratory, cornered me one afternoon at the Law Courts Building. He stressed the value of this innovative type of blood examination.

"We don't do DNA testing at our crime lab yet," he confided, "but I suggest that you try and get it done somewhere."

In the early autumn of 1989, after Brian Jack had been committed to stand trial for murder, I met with Assistant Commissioner J.B.D. Henry at Divisional Headquarters of The Royal Canadian Mounted Police.

He informed me that civilian personnel on staff at the R.M.C.P. Crime Lab in Ottawa were pioneering this new technology and the waiting list was long.

The commissioner was vaguely aware of the facts of the Jack case. I apprised him of the difficulties faced by the Prosecution in having to establish the fact of death without a body. I urged him to exert his influence in expediting the DNA testing because of the rare and unique circumstances in which we found ourselves.

You could have knocked me over with a Popsicle stick. He looked at me impassively and said, "It's a case of first come, first served."

In late July 1990, Assistant Commissioner R.A. Bergman, Director of the R.C.M.P. Forensic Laboratory Services in Ottawa, advised the court that the testing would be completed by mid-August. It wasn't. We went to trial without it. The horsemen had let us down badly.

❖ ❖ ❖ ❖ ❖

O'Sullivan implied that the jury was entitled to draw inferences unfavourable to the Crown because of its failure to furnish DNA test results.

For me, this irrational conclusion was but further confirmation of his well-recognized defence orientation.

He indicated, as previously stated, that Defence counsel was entitled to ask: Where were the witnesses who claimed to have seen Mrs. Jack after the alleged time of her death?

The investigative officers were satisfied that Christine Jack had not been seen after December 17, 1988.

My associate Kaplan and I, after diligent consideration, had come to the same conclusion.

Had it been otherwise, there would have been no need to call witnesses. Brian Jack would not have been prosecuted for murder.

❖ ❖ ❖ ❖ ❖

The O'Sullivan Concurrence

"Where was the young son of Mr. Jack, the son who must have seen material incidents on the night of the alleged disappearance?" queried the senior judge on the panel.

Because the Crown did not elect to put this six-year-old boy in the witness box, he suggested the jurors could infer that Adam would say something detrimental to the case for the Prosecution.

I doubt it would ever have occurred to the cynical O'Sullivan that some of the jurors might have drawn a favourable inference because the Jack children were not compelled to testify.

Suppose Kaplan and I had exposed Adam and Kairsten to the unfamiliar world of the courtroom? Imagine their reaction to the staring faces of a swarm of total strangers.

If we had subjected these children to the torment of a trial and the trauma of cross-examination, it would have been open to the jury to draw a very logical inference, that the Prosecutors were a pair of bastards who would stoop to doing anything to win.

❖ ❖ ❖ ❖ ❖

The Jack trial was not the first one in which I had been involved where O'Sullivan denigrated the Crown for its handling of a case. I had appeared before him in the Court of Appeal on numerous occasions over the years and had grown quite accustomed to his anti-Crown barbs.

This time, he seemed to begrudge the Crown its right to exercise its discretion in the selection of witnesses.

I found his reference to Brian Jack's young son, and the possible consequences of the Crown's failure to call him as a witness, unnecessary and irresponsible.

Brian Kaplan and I meditated long and hard over the advisability of having the children testify. Certainly they had witnessed things which, if disclosed, would have been highly prejudicial to the Defence.

Kaplan, by coincidence, was the father of a six-year-old son, the same age as Adam, and a daughter just a year younger than Kairsten. He was extremely apprehensive about the psychological effect a court appearance could have on children of such tender years, particularly in the circumstances of this case.

Early on, we had come to the conclusion that if Brian Jack were to be convicted, he would be convicted whether the children testified or not.

Before our ultimate decision was made, however, Brian was anxious to have a little chat with Adam and Kairsten.

Lidijia Jankovec made the arrangements.

Her old friend Veletei Reiter, Christine's mother, would bring her grandchildren over to visit Aunt Lidijia. Mr. Kaplan would just happen to drop in.

"After talking to the kids, I knew they could not assist the case one iota," my associate said. "I said to Mrs. Reiter, 'What would you say if I told you I wanted to call the kids to the stand to testify?' 'I would tell you exactly what Christine would have told you,' she replied. 'If you don't have to call them, don't.'"

We didn't.

Show me a man who has never made a slip of the tongue and I'll show you a man who doesn't have one.

—John Douglas Montgomery

The Second Trial

Dangerfield. Were I about to be prosecuted for murder by someone who bore the name Dangerfield, a sense of foreboding would surely overtake me.

But there was more to fear than the ominous name alone. J.G.B. Dangerfield stands well over six feet, a grizzled veteran of a quarter of a century in the criminal courts. He would lead the prosecution team this time.

Richard Saull, his junior at the Crown counsel table, is a little guy with a cherubic face, which belies his reputation as a scrapper.

It is not widely known, but in recent years he has become a certified professional boxing judge.

Walk into Rick Saull's office and you will see on display on top of a filing cabinet a large, framed photograph of Mohammed Ali with him.

It was during the Sugar Ray Leonard/Donny Lalonde fight at Caesar's Palace in Las Vegas a few years back that Rick met the champ. I don't know how tight they are today, but this much I do know: The champ is one of Rick's role models.

Dangerfield and Saull's cumulative prosecutorial experience exceeded 40 years at the time the second trial got under way on September 14, 1992.

I have observed that their style of advocacy is quite similar. Both are quick to anger and neither one is particularly tender in mercy. Tiger Wolson and his able lieutenant, John McAmmond, were in for some blistering skirmishes.

There was absolutely no doubt in my mind that once the dust of battle had finally settled, Brian Jack would take up residence in the federal institution at Stony Mountain.

At the time of Brian Jack's second trial, Mr. Justice Wallace M. Darichuk, the presiding judge, was possessed of an encyclopedic knowledge of the criminal law, amassed over 29 years on the bench.

The youthful Darichuk was appointed to the magisterial bench before he had turned 30. By the time of his appointment to the County Court, he had served as a police magistrate and Provincial Court Judge for 13 years. He was elevated to the Court of Queen's Bench in 1985.

None of the thorny legal issues that were bound to infest this trial would faze him. His vast experience in criminal jurisprudence would ensure that all the issues would be resolved fairly, and that counsel would not be permitted to struggle too far off course.

One of His Lordship's most admirable traits is his infinite courtesy to members of the bar. All counsel who appear before him are referred to as "learned counsel." I have heard him address in this fashion scores of lawyers over the years, whether they were bright and well-prepared or slothful and slightly daft.

Six men and six women would decide the fate of Brian Jack this time. Each one took the juror's oath on the opening day of the trial and then the jury was immediately dispatched for two weeks. That much time would be required to sort out the evidentiary problems that inevitably surface in a case of this complexity. They have to be dealt with without the jury present.

Much to my regret, I would be unable to sit in on the trial. I was totally occupied at that time with another murder trial. I did attend one morning session of the Jack trial, however, when the Crown tendered the long-awaited DNA evidence. After that, I gave no further thought to the trial of Brian Jack.

❖ ❖ ❖ ❖ ❖

The events of Saturday morning, October 31, 1992, spring sharply into focus. I went out to stock up on Halloween candy, as the little witches and ghosts and goblins would be at our door in a few short hours.

Just as I alighted from the car, a friend who was leaving the drug store where I was headed saw me and yelled. Then he began jabbing his right index finger in the direction of the two boxes which dispensed the *Winnipeg Free Press* and the *Winnipeg Sun*. They were located no more than 20 feet from where I had parked.

My curiosity was aroused. I wandered over to the newspaper dispensers. A big, black headline caught me squarely between the eyes:

JACK NOT GUILTY
WANTS KIDS BACK

Something obviously had gone wrong; very, very wrong. The *Sun*'s glaring revelation:

BRIAN JACK A FREE MAN

was proclaimed in two and three-quarter inch print.

A colourful snapshot of a smiling Christine Jack, with Kairsten in her arms and little Adam at her side, accompanied the caption. A large head-and-shoulders photograph of Brian Jack completed the sensational front page layout.

Years have passed since this unsettling moment. My memory of the instant, however, remains unclouded.

I dropped the correct change in the coin slots, picked up both dailies and walked across the street to a doughnut shop.

After having ordered coffee and a raisin bran muffin (I know this because I never deviate from raisin bran), I put on my glasses and read.

> With four years of emotion bottled inside him, Brian Jack sobbed uncontrollably, collapsing in the prisoner's box last night, after being declared not guilty of killing his wife, Christine.
>
> After the jury foreman read the verdict, Jack's lawyer, Richard Wolson, stood and made a bee-line for the tall, balding man, who reached out and tightly clutched the lawyer's hand.
>
> Colour flushing his face, Jack slumped forward, his body limp as he wept with his head and arms resting on the edge of the box, while the judge discharged the six men and six women who had handed him his freedom.
>
> Leaving the cubicle where he sat for seven weeks during his second trial and for 36 days during his first trial—which ended with a guilty verdict and a minimum ten-year prison term—he seemed barely able to stand, leaning on a chair for support.
>
> Wolson advised Jack not to talk to the media in his emotional state.

"I'm very happy for Brian. I am thrilled for Brian. He's been through a tremendous ordeal in the last four years. He's so emotional...He wants to gather his belongings and be on his way,'"Wolson said.[18]

Doughnut shop patrons were invited to clear their own tables. A garbage container with a disposal flap bearing the appreciative inscription "Thank you" was close by my table.

My partially consumed raisin bran muffin had suddenly lost its flavour. I crammed the remnants of my snack down the garbage shoot along with both newspapers. Had my practicing certificate been close at hand, I would have tossed it into the bin, too.

That morning, I would have willingly saddled up with the vigilantes.

❖ ❖ ❖ ❖ ❖

Why did the first jury convict Brian Jack of second-degree murder and the second jury acquit him?

What had brought about this inconceivable reversal?

The only significant difference in the evidence in the latter case involved the introduction of the DNA evidence. In the final analysis, the second trial was all but a replay of the first.

The Crown wasted no time in launching an appeal against Jack's acquittal. Unfortunately, Mr. Justice Darichuk had made an inadvertent but critical error. The jury had sought clarification as to the difference between second-degree murder and manslaughter and he had misdirected them. As a result, Brian Jack would stand trial for a third time.

A brief historical note may explain, in part, why things went awry for the prosecution.

After the Crown had closed its case and the Defence had elected to call no evidence, His Lordship embarked upon his charge to the jury. He spoke for approximately seven hours over the course of one and a half days, concluding at 5:30 p.m. on the second day (October 29, 1992). The court reconvened that evening, and several questions were put to the trial judge by the jury before it retired at 9:30 p.m. The next morning (October 30, 1992), the jury asked another question relating to a point of evidence and then resumed its deliberations. At approximately 4:00 p.m. the court reconvened to deal with the following questions from the jury:

Due to a stalemate in deliberations, we are requesting a further

The Second Trial

clarification about reasonable doubt in the case of circumstantial evidence and re-clarification as to the difference between second-degree murder and manslaughter.

The learned trial judge said to the jurors:

> Let me deal with the second part of this question, where you asked for a re-clarification as to the difference between second-degree murder and manslaughter.

Few judges I have known speak with greater precision or clarity than Wallace Darichuk. Lucidity is one of his trademarks. He answered:

> Essentially, murder, is killing by means of an unlawful act with specific intent…while manslaughter is killing by means of an unlawful act with this specific intent.

At that very moment the die was cast. His Lordship meant to say, "Manslaughter is killing by means of an unlawful act without this specific intent."

He continued:

> What was the specific intent that I referred you to? That the accused either meant to cause her death or meant to cause bodily harm that he knew was likely to cause death and was reckless about whether or not it caused death. So, you will see that basically the difference is one of intent.

Approximately 38 minutes later, the jury returned with a verdict of not guilty.

❖ ❖ ❖ ❖ ❖

Chief Justice Scott wrote:

> All counsel are agreed that the trial judge misspoke in his recharge respecting the difference between murder and manslaughter. He made an inadvertent error (characterized by counsel for the respondent as a Lapsus Linguae). He undoubtedly intended to use the word 'without' instead of the word 'with' when contrasting

the specific intent that is required to constitute the offence of murder, but not manslaughter.

The crucial issue before this Court is whether this error was fatal?[19]

From a very personal standpoint, I sympathized with Wally Darichuk. He was not given to slips of the tongue. But he made one. It cost the taxpayer plenty and he knew it. And he grieved about it.

So he screwed up. Who hasn't?

❖ ❖ ❖ ❖ ❖

Surely a terse "The trial judge made a fatal error. A new trial is ordered" would have sufficed. Instead, tortuous pages of judicial pedantry were churned out by the appellate division. As Chief Justice Scott was coming into the home stretch, he wrote:

> In my opinion, it is impossible to say that the members of the jury—had they been properly instructed—would have necessarily rendered a verdict of acquittal. The jurors asked the trial judge for help on a specific and critical area in the law. The advice they received was wrong. It is not tenable to suggest that in the verdict that followed almost immediately thereafter they ignored or recognized the error in the trial judge's slip of the tongue.

Finally, as he neared the finishing line, he noted:

> The last issue to be decided is whether the respondent should be retried on a charge of murder or manslaughter. The respondent argues that since the trial Judge plainly got it right with respect to the charge of murder, he has therefore been acquitted by a jury of his peers properly instructed with respect to that offence. He should therefore stand trial, if obliged to do so, on the reduced charge of manslaughter. In my opinion, there is merit to the respondent's position.
>
> There should be a new trial, but on a charge of manslaughter.

❖ ❖ ❖ ❖ ❖

It was ten months and ten days after his acquittal that the Court of Appeal

The Second Trial

ordained that Brian Jack would be tried again, albeit on the lesser count of manslaughter.

Then, on May 24, 1994, just one week shy of 20 months since his client's emancipation, the irrepressible Wolson stood before seven members of the nation's highest court. He was hell-bent on having them reverse the decision of the Scott tribunal. However, the Court of Last Resort rejected his spirited argument. It was confirmed: The beleaguered Jack would face yet another judge and another assize court jury.

A jury is a group of twelve people of average ignorance.
—Herbert Spencer

The Third Trial

To the courtroom born, both as advocate and jurist, that was John Ambrose Scollin. His legendary wit and wisdom throughout his sojourn at the bar and on the bench was a constant source of delight to the regulars in the gallery and an inspiration to those at the counsel tables. The announcement that he would preside at Brian Jack's third trial was greeted with sighs of relief from attorneys for the prosecution and defence alike.

It seems that every Crown attorney in the province wanted to scrimmage with Brian Jack. This time, Robert Clinton Morrison joined quarterback George Dangerfield on offence. He can be just as cantankerous as Dangerfield. He can be equally erudite and effective, too.

Young Morrison and I have worked together on at least three murder trials that I readily recall. Each time, he implored me to let him handle jury selection. I applauded his enthusiasm, attributing it solely to his dedication and quest for experience. My admiration for the lad's zeal obliterated all sense of what the crafty Morrison was up to. We always wound up with at least two very pretty ladies on our juries. There is little room for doubt, then, that the shameless plotter had offered his supposed expertise in the selection process to an unsuspecting Dangerfield.

The trial started in high gear on the morning of January 30, 1995. The jury, impaneled before noon, comprised seven women and five men. I had occasion to attend the trial for an hour or so one day. It took but a brief glance at the enclosure that housed the 12 triers of the facts to witness once again the handiwork of Robert Clinton Morrison.

Charter House waitress Shirley Garbutt was among the last of the 45 witnesses to testify. This lady had got under the skin of the placid Beanie

The Third Trial

Kaplan during the first trial. I wondered how she would react to the cross-examination by the more volatile Morrison. I sat in court during the prolonged and smoldering confrontation. Eventually, as she left the witness box, her eyes were glued to the redoubtable prosecutor. If looks could kill, it is a safe bet that Robert Morrison would be "at rest" in Chapel Lawn Memorial Gardens.

❖ ❖ ❖ ❖ ❖

The trial, though a lengthy one, was of much shorter duration than the first two. On the morning of February 28, at 11:45, members of the panel were consigned to the jury room to begin their deliberations. At 4:30 that afternoon, court reconvened as there were two perplexing questions to be answered: "Where was Earl Weber?" and "What happens if we can't agree?"

Mr. Justice Scollin assured the jurors that they need not concern themselves with the whereabouts of the witness Weber on the evening that Christine Jack disappeared.

He then informed them that it was far too early to be concerned about an impasse. Mildly, he urged them to "exercise good sense" and to try to reach a decision.

At 2:05 p.m. the following day, the jury returned to the courtroom. They brought with them neither glad tidings of great joy for the accused nor for his accusers. Their solemn countenances foreshadowed their plight. They had reached a deadlock. The foreman arose and addressed the Court.

"After reviewing all of the evidence thoroughly," he intoned, "we, the jury, cannot reach a unanimous decision."

Richard Wolson beseeched the trial judge to discharge the jury at this stage. His request was promptly denied.

The esteemed Justice Scollin was somewhat peeved when he wheeled his chair around to face the jurors. Testily, he urged them to endeavour to reach agreement.

Inevitably, his exhortation would be bisected, trisected and microscopically examined by judges of the appellate division and the Supreme Court of Canada. Regrettably, he would be judged by many, precious few of whom could have legitimately batted in his league.

Because his admonition formed the basis of the third appeal, this narrative would be incomplete without its inclusion.

To the jury he said:

In my view, I reviewed the issues thoroughly for you. Although there were 45 witnesses and a number of exhibits, the issues are brutally simple. You have two women claiming that they saw Christine Jack alive, in a restaurant, on her own, on December 23, six days after her disappearance. Not a word has been heard from her in six years, neither by children, by parents or by friends.

Was this woman in the red coat, who looked like Christine Jack, in fact Christine Jack? Do not isolate and try to decide this issue as if there were no other material evidence to be considered.

Consider it. Can you rationally, in the light of the other evidence you have heard, accept this proposition? If you accept it, as I've told you, you must acquit. If you have a reasonable doubt, you must acquit. But before deciding whether the doubt you have on this or any other aspect of the case is reasonable, do take the evidence and place it in the context of the whole case. Place it in the context of the other evidence which points to her disappearance being explained only by death on December 17.

I warn you again not to take any piece of evidence, good, bad or indifferent, in isolation. Before you come to consider whether a doubt about the identification of Christine Jack is a reasonable doubt, go through the exercise I suggested that you do. There is ample evidence for you to decide that. Ample evidence that this Blazer, driving east and west on the highway, was the Jack Blazer. There is ample evidence, if you accept it, of identification of the accused in association with that Blazer on that night. How many Blazers of this sort, with stains of blood, are likely to be driving around at night?

These are 'likelies.' How likely is it that the witnesses who individually and separately purported to identify the accused were mistaken? What inferences do you draw about anonymous phone calls? These and other questions that arise should not be beyond the bounds of reasonable people to consider and decide upon.

I have said before, and I say again, that in their deliberations jurors do not leave their common sense hanging on the peg along with their coat. Avoid trying to be amateur investigators. Avoid being spectators. You're not called here to try and be Sherlock Holmes. Stick to the evidence that you have and, with good will, apply your common sense and debate the issues honestly and fairly.

If you are in a minority, explain what you see is the logic of your position, based only on the evidence, and listen and pay attention to the views of those who do not agree with you.

If, after serious further debate along these lines, your views remain as they may be, so be it. But I urge you, do not lightly disagree and risk exposing this accused and the justice system to a further presentation of the same evidence before 12 other people at some later time.

A reasonable doubt arises only from rational consideration, not from insecure, fanciful or unfounded musings.

If you have such a doubt, fine; you know what to do—acquit. If you don't, then you convict. If on the whole of the evidence you find it proved beyond a reasonable doubt the accused drove the Blazer that night, then he certainly told a pack of lies to police and to friends. Why? You know, answer the whole question. But it's the kind of thing you should ask yourself. Apply your minds to that, make a decision on it, and the rest of the evidence will likely fall into place.

God gave you all, in varying degrees, the power to reason. Use it. It is possible that the source of disagreement is a misunderstanding of the evidence or the law. If you do have any difficulty in analyzing the testimony and need your memories refreshed for the purposes of debate, you let me know. And in consultation with counsel, I'll give you what further advice I can. But in the meantime, carry on and do your very best as your oath requires you.[20]

With that, the jury again retired to continue its deliberations. The instant the last juror had disappeared from view, a much agitated Tiger Wolson sprang to his feet.

"In essence this is a charge to convict the accused!" he admonished the somewhat startled Scollin. "And with respect to reasonable doubt, you've put it to them in an essence that is absolutely oriented towards the Crown."

I chanced to have been in court during the trial judge's attempt to avoid a deadlock. I heard his exhortation in an entirely different key than that of the prisoner's counsel.

Francis Bacon, the English philosopher, essayist and statesman, who fell off the perch way back in the year 1626, would have approved of John Ambrose Scollin's instruction. Bacon, a one-time solicitor general and Lord Chancellor of England, was heard to say to a new judge:

"You shall be a light to new jurors to open their eyes, not a guide to lead them by the noses."[21]

At 10:15 a.m. the next day, March 2, 1995, the jury returned with a unanimous verdict of guilty of manslaughter. Some time before a consensus had been reached, the foreman of the jury had been replaced.

The penalty was promptly imposed.

"I think the ends of justice will be satisfied with a sentence of four years," Mr. Justice Scollin said, noting that the killing appeared to be an isolated incident by a non-violent man.

"It was, in my view, an assault that went tragically, tragically wrong," the judge observed. "His own life is now wasted because of this tragic, unintended death."

❖ ❖ ❖ ❖ ❖

The Crown had asked for a 20-year sentence. The Defence had suggested two to three years. Both factions were dissatisfied. A third appeal was inevitable.

Much Ado About Nothing
The Third Appeal—Part One

Four hundred and seventy-three days. Four hundred and seventy-three days from verdict to verification. No matter how ingenious the rationalization might be, such a time span is unconscionable.

Brian Jack was convicted of manslaughter on the second day of March 1995. The first installment of his third appeal was not heard until June 17, 1996, 473 days later. Judgment was reserved.

The judges of the Court of Appeal, unfettered by periods of statutory limitations, can hover over their opinions at a leisurely pace if they are so inclined. A hundred more days would pass before the court would render its judgment.

The issues for Their Lordships to resolve were, as well, to borrow from the insightful prose of the learned trial judge, "brutally simple," so much so, in my less than humble opinion, that they could have been put to rest and the judgment concluded in fewer than 15 minutes.

Chief Justice Scott delved into the written opinions of a host of judicial luminaries who had expanded upon the ground rules for a flawless exhortation. He shared snippets of these pronouncements in his own somewhat wordy discourse:

> On the first question, whether the trial judge's language coerced the jury into reaching a unanimous decision, I find no merit in the appellant's submission.
>
> The trial judge's language in this case was not restrained. Indeed, the trial judge used colourful language throughout the trial. His strong language in the exhortation is consistent with his manner of speech both in and out of the jury's presence. The exhortation does not represent a marked departure in his communication

style to which the jury had been exposed. The exhortation was not tainted by the trial judge's use of the phrases "brutally simple'"or "can you rationally...accept" or "stains of blood" or "pack of lies." While it would have been preferable for him to have avoided any language which could be regarded as inflammatory or influential, I conclude that the quoted phrases alone could not and did not influence the jury or affect their freedom to deliberate.

Even chief justices might occasionally heed the admonition of the Augustinian monk, Martin Luther, who reminded all of us that "The fewer words, the better prayer."

Chief Justice Scott lumbered on:

I commence by stating that it is my view that in the circumstances of this case the trial judge was quite entitled to conduct a concise review of the facts. When the jury indicated that they had "thoroughly reviewed the facts" but were still deadlocked, this was an open invitation for the trial judge to "take the bull by the horns" and point out to the jury that analysis of the evidence before them was not necessarily a complex and difficult task. The trial judge was entirely justified in making a brief review of the most significant points in the evidence that the jury had to advert to. In these circumstances, the trial judge correctly relied on his experience and instinct and did not step over the line in so doing. Consistent with what he had done throughout, he spoke bluntly and plainly.[23]

Consistent with what I have done throughout, namely selective judge-bashing, I will continue to write bluntly and plainly.

How refreshing it would have been if, for once, the chief justice had shelved his judicial purism and written bluntly and plainly, perhaps something like, "There wasn't a bloody thing wrong with that exhortation, Mr. Wolson, and your appeal is dismissed."

❖ ❖ ❖ ❖ ❖

Mr. Justice Charles Huband and Madam Justice Bonnie Helper were the other members of the Scott triumvirate who would decide the fate of the hapless Jack.

A mini-biographical sketch of these jurists appeared in a *Winnipeg Free Press* piece entitled, "Meet the Seven Who Make the Rulings."

Much Ado About Nothing, The Third Appeal—Part One

Charles Huband

Leader of the provincial grits in the mid-1970s, Huband is also seen as having liberal views on the bench, which he joined without prior judicial apprenticeship in 1979.

The former civil litigator is regarded as an intellectual, in part because of his teaching at the University of Manitoba law school.

While lawyers say he is a pleasure to appear before, they say his decisions can sometimes be unpredictable. One lawyer said she feels Huband has not fulfilled the high expectations that accompanied his appointment.

Bonnie Helper

Helper made Manitoba legal history in 1989 when she became the first woman to sit on this high court. She had been in the Court of Queen's Bench Family Division since 1983 and prior to that was a Provincial Court Family Judge since 1978.

She's not regarded as a feminist and is seen as being at the conservative end of the spectrum. The only Jewish member of the court at the time of her elevation, Helper won the gold medal in law at the U of M in 1966.[24]

It was a house divided. While Mr. Justice Huband concurred with Chief Justice Scott's decision to dismiss the appeal, Madam Justice Helper dissented. She concluded that the trial judge had failed to conduct his exhortation in a "balanced and fair way." Thus, she would have allowed the appeal and set aside the conviction.

I was more determined than ever to leave the Department of Justice and retire to a sheep ranch in New Mexico, after having read the forty-eighth paragraph of Chief Justice Scott's judgment in the first part of this third appeal in which he stated:

> At the request of counsel for the accused, the Court has not dealt with the question whether a judicial stay of proceedings ought to be entered should the appeal be allowed on the basis that to subject the accused to a fourth trial would be manifestly unfair, if not unprecedented. Although it is my view that all matters pertaining to the conviction appeal should have been addressed at one hearing, in view of the fundamental importance of this issue, I agree

with the appellant's request to reconvene the hearing for the purposes of hearing argument on this point.

Sixty-one more days. Sixty-one days until November 25, 1996, when the same panel of judges would reconvene to hear the balance of the appeal.

How fervently lawyers and judges espouse the old maxim, "Justice delayed is justice denied." In practice, however, it seems to have far greater application to some other guy's case than to their own.

❖ ❖ ❖ ❖ ❖

If we lived in a Utopian society, there would be a court of criminal appeal to deal with the likes of Brian Jack. Those who graced that bench would have won their spurs as advocates in the criminal courts. The best among them would ascend to the trial division to preside over major criminal trials. Then, as venerable members of that appellate court either retired or having given up the ghost, there would always be qualified replacements waiting in the wings.

But what profiteth a man to live on Dream Street? There is no court of criminal appeal. Perhaps it will emerge in the third millenium. In the meantime, we bungle on.

❖ ❖ ❖ ❖ ❖

Vivacious, fashionably elegant, brilliant and just a downright lovely lady—that is Madam Justice Bonnie Helper. In her field of expertise—family law—she is supreme. However, in my lofty opinion she is no more qualified to sit in judgment of John Ambrose Scollin on matters of criminal law than I am to fly a 747.

Back in the mid-sixties, while she was still distinguishing herself academically, John Scollin had become firmly established as a most respected advocate in the Supreme Court of Canada. I can personally attest to this, having seen him in action before the judges of that court on at least five separate and distinct occasions. And what a court it was in those days! Judicial giants all—Fauteux, Abbott, Martland, Judson, Ritchie, Spence, Hall, Pigeon and Laskin. I witnessed the great deference paid to him and the rapt attention his submissions received.

I hasten to add that from agonizing personal experience, not all mortals who appeared before that august body received the same warm reception accorded John Ambrose Scollin. He had been Deputy Minister of Justice,

Much Ado About Nothing, The Third Appeal—Part One

but soon wearied of administrative functions and happily returned to the courtroom as Chief General Counsel for the Federal Department of Justice.

With his vast experience as a barrister, particularly in the realm of criminal law, his appointment as a judge of the Court of Queen's Bench was greeted with marked enthusiasm. He fast developed a multitude of devoted followers among counsel for the Crown and for the Defence.

I still shake my head in wonderment when I reflect upon the credentials of those who deigned to pass judgment on the Scollin exhortation.

> *Courts must have the respect and support of the community in order that the administration of criminal justice may properly fulfill its function.*
> —Madam Justice L'Heureux-Dubé

The Third Appeal—Part Two

The anxiously awaited second installment of the third appeal was delivered on December 11, 1996.

I got hold of a copy on December 12, holed up in my den, read it over and over and then brooded for the next two hours. During this period of mournful meditation, I harkened back to the words of the, "The Rabbit"— "Some of you guys would have been better off enroling in Molar's Barber College or learning a trade at R.B. Russell school."

Just about then, I wished to hell I had.

And I reflected, too, upon the bench. The workbench, I thought with mounting cynicism, would have been a more appropriate destination for some of them, as well.

❖ ❖ ❖ ❖ ❖

It will be remembered, or maybe it won't, that the court reconvened to hear argument on two issues respecting which argument had been postponed at the time of the initial hearing. The issues were first, whether it was an abuse of process—in the event that the trial judge's exhortation should be found to have exceeded permissible limits—for the accused to be placed in jeopardy by way of a fourth trial; and second, the Crown's appeal from the sentence of four years' imprisonment imposed by the trial judge.

"What the hell is this 'abuse of process' crap all about?" a good friend of mine, an untutored layman, queried venomously. "I still don't get it. I thought this case was all about the abuse of a wife, not a process."

❖ ❖ ❖ ❖ ❖

To constitute an abuse of process and a violation of the Canadian Charter of Rights and Freedoms sufficient to require a stay of criminal proceedings, the ultimate test was enunciated by the Supreme Court of Canada in 1985.

It stipulated: "Where compelling an accused to stand trial would violate those fundamental principles of justice which underline the community's sense of fair play and decency, or where the proceedings are oppressive, this is a power which can be exercised, but only in the clearest of cases."

Observed Chief Justice Scott:

> Not suprisingly, I have been unable to find any case in which a court has allowed a fourth trial for an indictable offence to proceed in the face of an application either at common law or under the Charter for a judicial stay of proceedings. In my opinion, it would be a very rare case indeed where putting an accused in jeopardy with respect to a serious charge for the fourth time would not constitute a breach of the Charter, and an abuse of process sufficient to warrant a judicial stay of proceedings.

With a cumbersome 119-word sentence, the Chief Justice plodded on:

> In this case, the extensive delay since the disappearance of Christine Jack, amounting now to almost eight years; the fact that a further appeal to the Supreme Court is a certainty, resulting in even more delay; the fact that the accused has not contributed in any significant way to the passage of time other than by the exercise of his rights of appeal (whereas the Crown did by its conduct contribute to the delay in proceeding with the first trial); together with the impact which a fourth trial could have on all those involved in the proceedings, to say nothing of the respect for the judicial process itself, all lead me to conclude that to proceed would tarnish the image of the court.

Had the Chief Justice conducted a survey of the men and women in the courthouse corridors, he would have discovered a great many who concluded that to not proceed would tarnish the image of the court.

As he drew nigh unto the completion of this segment of his judgment, Chief Justice Scott adopted the words of Madam Justice L'Heureux-Dubé in support of his decision:

> Courts must have the respect and support of the community, in order that the administration of criminal justice may properly fulfill its function. Consequently, where the affront to fair play and decency is disproportionate to the societal interest in the effective prosecution of criminal cases, then the administration of justice is best served by staying the proceedings."

The Chief Justice announced that "this was such a case. Had I determined that the verdict of the jury at the third trial of the accused should be set aside, I would have ordered a judicial stay of proceedings pursuant to the Charter.

The odds were now 76 to three that Brian Jack would never again darken a prison doorway. I forced myself to read on, however, because I was curious to learn what the Scott court would have deemed an appropriate punishment on the off chance that the sentence were to be carried out.

Amid my chronic carping and judge-bashing, I have to confess that I found momentary solace when I read:

> In my opinion, the sentence of four years imposed by the trial judge is unfit. It fails to account for the facts as found by the sentencing judge which, but for the special circumstances already noted, bring it close to the "high end" of sentences to be imposed following a conviction for manslaughter. In all of the circumstances I would allow the Crown's sentence appeal and increase the sentence from one of four years to six. In so concluding, I wish to make it clear that the sentence would have been substantially higher were it not for the lengthy delay and the resulting adverse impact upon the accused.

And speaking of lengthy delays, there would be yet another one.

One hundred and ninety-one days. That's how much time would drag by before the Court of Last Resort's final determination of the fate of Brian Gordon Jack.

There is but one blasphemy, and that is injustice.
—Robert Ingersoll

The Supreme Court—A Post-Mortem

The Supreme Court set Brian Jack free.

On June 20, 1997, eight and a half years after his victim had vanished from the face of the earth, five judges of the nine-member court let him go.

Thomas Jefferson said that the sword of the law should never fall but on those whose guilt is so apparent as to be pronounced by their friends as well as foes.

Brian Jack's guilt was apparent to two juries. His guilt was apparent to many of his friends and also to a few former friends, who confided in me over the years. And, yet, the sword of the law in the case of *Regina v. Brian Gordon Jack* remained unsheathed by the then Chief Justice of Canada and four members of his court.

Chief Justice Lamer orally delivered the judgment of the court. It would have taken him no more than a minute and a half to recite it. Its entire content is encapsulated in ten lines in the Supreme Court Reports.

In a nutshell, he said that the majority of the court was in substantial agreement with Madam Justice Helper's dissent, that the appeal was allowed and that a new trial was ordered.

I have read many Solomonic judgments in my time which have enhanced the rule of law. Wise and noble judges have striven to perpetuate our concept of justice. They have succeeded admirably without the aid of the Canadian Charter of Rights and Freedoms. An innate respect for the sanctity of human life and an appreciation of the value of condigned punishment always prevailed.

I was proud and honoured to have had a miniscule part to play in the administration of criminal justice. It filled me with a sense of fulfillment and exaltation. But that was yesterday.

In his ruling on the Jack case the Chief Justice said:

> The appellant has asked for a stay of proceedings given the numerous trials and appeals the accused has been subjected to. Since the Court of Appeal of Manitoba gave reasons with which we are in full agreement, that they would have entered a stay had the majority allowed the appeal, a stay is therefore entered.

These words failed to exalt me. I sorely wanted to vomit.

❖ ❖ ❖ ❖ ❖

Few judges I have known were possessed of the wit, wisdom and audaciousness of Mr. Justice Scollin.

When a young lawyer cited a precedent-setting 1984 decision of the Supreme Court to bolster her argument, the right arm of the jurist was thrust forward at shoulder level, reminiscent of a traffic cop on point duty. He stopped her in her tracks. "It was a retrogressive decision," he chided. "I have no hesitation in saying it is a decision arrived at by a court which does in fact lack adequate training and experience in criminal law."

It was this court, lacking in adequate training and experience in criminal law, that emancipated Brian Jack.

The Scollin denunciation of the decision to which counsel had referred was memorable. I have adopted his words as my own in my personal condemnation of the Supreme Court decision in the Jack case.

I have no hesitation in saying that it is an inadequate, poor, retrogressive decision arrived at in a way that will not stand up to the proper application and philosophy of the criminal law.

❖ ❖ ❖ ❖ ❖

The killer served 14 months in pre-trial custody prior to his first conviction. To the best of my knowledge, that was the full extent of the time he spent behind bars. And, yet, his counsel prattled on and on about the distress Brian Jack had suffered during the eight and a half years since the disappearance of his wife. He bemoaned the severe restrictions that had been placed upon his client's freedom while he was out on bail, not to mention his inability to obtain meaningful employment, and the difficulties he faced in communicating with his children.

But the salient question which begs to be asked is simply this: Does 14 months' imprisonment, coupled with certain restraints on one's freedom on the outside, adequately atone for taking the life of a human being?

Five judges of the Supreme Court of Canada, all vitally aware of the facts of this case, thought so.

❖ ❖ ❖ ❖ ❖

The beloved Aunt Lidijia Jankovec said that Christine's parents, Stephan and Veletei Reiter, were devastated by the rulings of the Supreme Court.

"The kids don't want to be anywhere near him," she added, referring to their father.

Antonio Lamer had drawn the final curtain on this nefarious courtroom drama. The case of *Regina v. Jack* was now just another closed file in the archives of the Department of Justice.

But there would never be closure for the family, friends and colleagues of Christine Jack, people who had loved her and admired her so much. Their loss was irreplaceable.

Hearts ache for Adam and Kairsten. Who could ever know the hurt these children have had to endure? Christine's parents have loved them and nourished them and watched over them ever since their mother was taken from them.

In writing this chapter, I have thought a great deal about Stephan and Veletei Reiter. They have borne this great human tragedy with forbearance and quiet dignity.

When parents bury a child, the agony they must suffer transcends human comprehension. But when parents know a child is dead, and yet have been deprived of that sacred moment to say goodbye, the hurt is everlasting.

Christine lies in an unmarked location, known only to the one who placed her there.

There is no memorial. There is no place to visit. And remember: There is no place, then, in which to cherish the memories, to honour a loved one's life, or for a child to leave a flower.

The Reiters suffered not one loss but two. They lost a beloved daughter and they lost, as well, respect for the administration of criminal justice in Canada, something which only intensified their sorrow.

Our justice system failed the Reiters and the Jankovecs and the MacMillans and the Henrys and all the other friends but, most of all, it failed Christine Jack.

Epilogue

In 1945, a quarter and a label from a tin of Beehive Golden Corn Syrup got you a photograph of your favourite N.H.L. hockey players. It was the same deal for a printed reproduction of the Sportsman's Creed.

Enshrined within the galaxies of hockey stars and countless other young jocks plastered all over my bedroom walls, the rules of the game by Grantland Rice were posted:

> For when the one great scorer comes
> To write against your name,
> He marks—Not that you won or lost—
> But how you played the game.[25]

Maybe the Corn Syrup Hall of Fame offerings were a little before Brian Jack's time. However, an old jock like himself would, no doubt, have read some of Rice's accounts of gridiron battles in *Sports Illustrated*. And perhaps he might have come across the verse concerning the one great scorer.

In any event, from everything I have gleaned about him, I am convinced that there was a day when Brian Jack did subscribe to such a code of honour.

But then something went dreadfully wrong. He began to play by a different set of rules; rules that involved some pretty rough play. And suddenly, completely out of character, he became a liar and a coward.

An old pal of mine, Dr. Les, a kindly physician, never fails to remind me that every day above ground is a bonus. Amen. Each sunrise brings the promise of a new day, a fresh start, opportunities for adventure and discovery, a time for renewed faith and strength and hope.

But not for Brian Jack.

With the dawning, there must come a recurring, gnawing, debilitating, soul-destroying, hellish awareness that he killed the woman he loved, his wife Christine, the mother of his son and daughter.

He can never escape the torment of his brutality nor the shame of his insidious lies.

He is a loser, big time.

His wife, his kids and his self-respect are all gone now. He must be the saddest, loneliest, most guilt-ridden mortal on the planet.

God knows, he really fumbled the ball. Nevertheless, by dint of judicial intervention, he wasn't tossed out of the big game.

The governors of the justice league, through its chief commissioner Antonio Lamer, decreed that no further penalties would be imposed.

Kaplan, Dangerfield, Saull, Morrison and I, his prosecutors, all got benched.

I'm on the sidelines now, and I am not vying for the job of spiritual advisor to Brian Jack. But I hope that I run into him one of these days. Ever since the Supreme Court's decision to enter a stay of judicial proceedings was announced, I have yearned for our paths to cross once again. They just might. Sergeant Schinkel tells me that he is still around town.

I want to tell him that I know that he can't recover the fumbled ball. But I want to suggest a step toward a partial recovery for him, and a lessening of the pain for the loved ones of his victim, as well. I want to say to him with all the fervor and fire and passion that this old prosecutor can summon:

> Look, Brian. You're not the only one who fumbled the ball. So did judges of our superior courts. If they hadn't, you would have paid dearly for your crime. But that's ancient history. You're free to walk wherever you choose. But I want to suggest a step in the direction of partial redemption for yourself. If you take it, it is bound to ease the pain for Christine's loved ones, too. Lead someone to the place where Christine lies!

Appendix

Crown Counsel's Closing Address

May it please My Lord, ladies and gentlemen of the jury:
There were times when Brian Jack spoke the unvarnished truth. There were times when he spoke only half truths. Sometimes he was a complete stranger to the truth. There were times when he was a bare-faced liar.
An eminent Canadian jurist, the late Mr. Justice McInnes, once said:

> There is, too often, a misconception as to the purpose of a criminal trial. It is sometimes regarded as a contest between the person making the complaint and the person accused; or between the police officer or Prosecutor who is conducting the prosecution and the accused person. This is far from the truth. What we are all seeking, and what we must be seeking, is the truth of what actually occurred; and so a criminal trial is not really a contest at all. It is, more properly, a solemn inquiry, conducted under certain specific rules, whereby it is sought to ascertain the truth of what actually occurred.

And it is for you, the ladies and gentlemen of the jury, to ascertain the truth about what actually occurred in the family room of the Jack residence at 170 Alburg Drive some time after a quarter to eight and before ten o'clock on Saturday night, December 17, 1988.
Further, it is for you to ascertain the truth about what transpired subsequently, insofar as both the victim and the accused were concerned.
You will recall the testimony of Constable Jay Paquette, the young officer from the Youth Division attached to the Missing Persons Section.
On Thursday, December 22, 1988, at about nine a.m., he attended at the Jack residence to ascertain from Mr. Jack whether anything new had

come to light or whether he had received any information with regard to his missing wife.

The officer stated that he took notes as Mr. Jack spoke and that he recorded his comments verbatim.

I ask you to recall with me the things that Brian Jack told Constable Paquette:

> We put the kids to bed. After that, we came down to the family room and started discussing our marriage problems.
>
> She told me that she couldn't live with me anymore. She said that she hated the sight of me and had trouble being in the same room, which was funny because we had a good sex life even up to a few days before she left.
>
> She brought up the fact that the house was in her name and she wanted me to move out. I told her that I wanted to work out our differences.
>
> You know, we saw a marriage counsellor and I felt it was doing some good.
>
> She said, "No way," it was over.
>
> I asked her where I would go. I don't have a job since I went out of business. I am lining up a job right now but I don't have it yet. I haven't been able to get down there because I've been sick. I told her I had no money and I wanted her to wait until I could get a job in the new year and then I would leave if things didn't work out.

Up to this point, ladies and gentlemen, what Mr. Jack had told Constable Paquette was the unvarnished truth.

But sometimes, Brian Jack was a stranger to the truth.

The next thing he said to Constable Paquette was, I suggest, just one more of the countless bare-faced lies he told to the many witnesses who testified before you:

> She got up, grabbed her winter coat and purse and left. She got into our truck and drove off.

The accused said that it was a yellow 1983 GMC Blazer, with 482 DGK was the plate number.

Brian Jack then said: "I didn't know what to do and I just waited around the house."

Appendix

No, ladies and gentlemen, that's not what happened. Christine Jack did not get up, grab her winter coat and purse and drive off in the Blazer. The dead do not rise up and walk out to the garage.

Christine Jack was killed in the family room of her home at 170 Alburg Drive on Saturday night, December 17, 1988.

There was one eyewitness to the tragic death of this young woman— her husband, the one who killed her, Brian Gordon Jack.

❖ ❖ ❖ ❖ ❖

You and you alone are the sole judges of the facts. The responsibility of determining the guilt or innocence of the accused is in your hands. Your task is a difficult one.

Many years ago, an old friend gave me a splendid book entitled *The Mind of a Juror*, written by a celebrated trial lawyer.

Whenever I start meditating upon what I am about to say to the members of the jury in a trial such as this, I pull the treasured volume down from a bookshelf, just as I did this past weekend.

And I made a note of two paragraphs which I would like to share with you because I think they sum up the jurors' difficult task:

> Jurors are expected to discover not only the errors or the perjury of the witnesses, but also the errors and fallacy of the lawyers which are even more puzzling; and it thus clearly appears that the most difficult work in the courtroom is given to the jurors. The proceedings are conducted on the assumption that the jurors' knowledge, shrewdness, mental power and agility, experience in affairs, knowledge of human nature and his sense of honour will lead him to decide correctly which contestant is right and which lawyer is correct in all kinds of the most complicated controversies.
>
> It is the wise juror's business to come into court and sit quietly and say nothing and to hear the witnesses and the arguments of the lawyers, and to decide on which side there is an abundance of proof. Notwithstanding the conflicting and the plausible but directly opposed arguments of skillful lawyers, he is expected to render a correct verdict in all kinds of the most complicated controversies.
>
> When the jurors' task is thus described, it is plain to see that this task is far from an easy one.[26]

I have watched you, ladies and gentlemen, during the course of this trial. The close attention you paid to the testimony of all of the witnesses is most gratifying; and I am satisfied that each and every one of you is equal to the difficult task to which you have been assigned.

All of the evidence has been placed before you. You have seen the witnesses. You have heard the testimony of each and every one of them as they stood in the box before you. Shortly, you will be asked to retire to consider your verdict; but before you do so, it is my duty to make certain observations that support the case which the Crown has made out against the accused and to interpret the evidence as I see it.

Since it is one of My Lord's functions to instruct you on the law, I must confine myself to a consideration of the facts. You will recall my having said to you at the outset of this trial that nothing that I was about to say to you was evidence, nor could be construed by you as evidence in this case, and that the evidence that you were to concern yourselves with was the evidence which came from the mouths of the witnesses.

Now, just as then, I urge upon you to consider what I am about to say to you not as evidence, since I am only placing before you the interpretation which I feel that the evidence reveals insofar as the case against the accused is concerned.

You are not bound to accept my interpretation of the evidence, just as you are not bound to accept that of my learned friend, Mr. Wolson or, for that matter, that of My Lord.

However, if you conclude that the Crown's interpretation has merit and is in accord with your own personal feelings, then such interpretation can be adopted by you as your own in your deliberations toward the reaching of a verdict.

But above all, I want you to remember that ultimately it will be your interpretation, your decision and your verdict based on the evidence.

You will again be told that the onus of proving the guilt of the accused lies on the Crown, and that this onus is not discharged until you are satisfied beyond a reasonable doubt of the guilt of the accused.

Ladies and gentlemen, the Crown alleges that Brian Gordon Jack, on or about the seventeenth day of December, in the year of Our Lord one thousand, nine hundred and eighty-eight, at the City of Winnipeg, in the Province of Manitoba, did unlawfully kill Christine Anna Jack and did thereby commit murder in the second degree.

In this case, the Crown must prove certain specific elements which constitute the crime of second-degree murder.

One of these elements is the fact of death; that is, that Christine Jack is dead.

Appendix

You have heard that despite exhaustive efforts by scores of police officers, to find a body, the body of Christine Jack has not been found.

I am sure that My Lord will tell you that at the trial of a person charged with murder, the fact of death is provable by circumstantial evidence, notwithstanding that neither the body nor any trace of the body has been found and that the accused has made no confession of any participation in the crime. However, before he can be convicted, the fact of death should be proved by such circumstances as render the commission of the crime certain and leave no ground for reasonable doubt; that is, the circumstantial evidence should be so cogent and compelling as to convince you 11 citizens that upon no rational hypothesis other than murder can the facts be accounted for.

Christine Jack literally disappeared from the face of the earth on Saturday night, the seventeenth of December, 1988.

Since that time, she has sent no word or message of any sort to her parents or friends, with all of whom she was on affectionate terms.

You may find it extraordinary that her father and mother and her dearest friends, those who loved her and whom she loved, have not heard from her since December of 1988.

You may find it extraordinary that Christine, whose great love for her children and whose devotion to them was so much a part of her being, would not have made any sort of contact with Adam and Kairsten over the past 22 months.

If there were merely the disappearance of Christine Jack and nothing more, your common sense would tell you how dangerous it would be to convict the accused of murder on such evidence.

But Christine Jack's unexplained disappearance is but one of a multitude of facts so incriminating, I suggest to you, as to be reasonably explicable only by an act of muder.

Oh, it is open to my learned friend, despite all of the evidence to the contrary, to contend that Christine might still be alive and have left the country; alternatively, that in the depths of her despair over a crumbling marriage, she might have taken her own life.

My learned friend will constantly remind you, I am certain, that because there is no proof of a corpus delecti, what you are left with at the end of the day is nothing more than conjecture and suspicion.

And he will over and over again press the point that the Crown is asking you to convict a man on a flimsy foundation of fanciful guesswork, of supposition and imagery conjured up in the minds of a couple of overzealous Crown attorneys.

I would like to make this very clear at the outset, ladies and gentlemen. No law officer of the Crown will ever ask a jury to convict a man on the basis of conjecture or speculation or suspicion.

What a sorry day it would be for the administration of criminal justice if a finding of guilt was based on anything but the clearest evidence.

Mr. Wolson may tell you that I am asking you to indulge in conjecture and speculation as to the fate of Christine Jack, to indulge in guesswork.

No, ladies and gentlemen; all I ask you to do is to draw logical inferences, and common sense conclusions from the proven facts.

Just incidentally, I have a feeling in my bones that while Mr. Wolson will continuously caution you against falling prey to conjecture and guesswork, he will indulge in some rather wild speculation himself, particularly when he deals with Christine's relationship with Earl Weber, a subject I shall return to after a while.

I know that when My Lord instructs you on the law as it pertains to circumstantial evidence, he will talk to you about logical inferences which can be drawn from proven facts…so I shall move on.

Christine Reiter married Brian Jack on August 23, 1980. Their son Adam was born on January 29, 1982; their daughter Kairsten on October 26, 1983.

They lived in a very nice house, a four-level split in a pleasant neighbourhood in a suburb of Winnipeg.

There can be no doubt but that Brian Jack loved his wife and children very, very much.

Unfortunately, serious marital problems developed in 1988.

By early December, the relationship had deteriorated to the extent that Christine wanted Brian to leave.

You will recall Lidijia Jankovec, Aunt Lidijia, testifying that Brian telephoned her on December 8 and asked for help in patching the troubled marriage: "He told me that he loved her very much and that life without her would be nothing," Tante Lidijia said.

And you will recall Tante Lidijia saying that Christine had called her from work one morning between December 10 and 14 and told her that she couldn't live with Brian any more, that "there is no more love, not even hate; just emptiness"? On cross-examination Mrs. Jankovec repeated to Mr. Wolson what Brian had said to her that life without Christine would be no life for him.

Brian Jack knew that his life with Christine was finished. "She hated the sight of me and had trouble being in the same room," he told Constable Paquette, you will remember.

Appendix

Brian Jack loved Christine.

And he knew that without her love for him, life had lost its meaning.

If he couldn't have her love and share her life, then nobody could. And so, he destroyed her.

Back on Monday morning, September the tenth, when I was privileged to make an opening statement, I said to you, "It is the position of the Crown that Christine Anna Jack is dead and that Brian Gordon Jack is responsible for her death; that he had the opportunity to kill her and a motive for so doing."

During our trial preparation, Mr. Kaplan and I were always vitally aware that the very first thing that you ladies and gentlemen of the jury would have to determine was whether Christine Jack was, in fact, dead.

Every criminal prosecution proceeds on the basis that an offence has been committed. The prosecutors must prove the offence and then prove that the accused committed it.

Well, how does the Crown establish that an offence has been committed? How does it establish the fact of Christine Jack's death? It does so by presenting, in evidence before you, the concurrence of so many separate facts and circumstances—themselves established beyond all reasonable doubt—all pointing to the fact of Christine Jack's death on or about the seventeenth of December, 1988.

We decided that it would be extremely helpful to you in your deliberations if we could help you to get to know Christine, to know her as a child, to know her as a young woman in her college days at Grand Forks, to know her as a speech therapist working with children with speech impediments. We wanted you to get to know Christine Jack, the industrious homemaker, the wife and the mother.

We wanted you, as far as humanly possible, to be in a position to decide for yourselves whether it was logical and reasonable to infer that Christine Jack had eloped with another man; or whether she just callously abandoned her children; or whether, in a moment of depression, she took her own life; or whether her husband killed her in the family room of their own home.

You may find that through the testimony of Cheryl MacMillan and Donna Mae Henry and Aunt Lidijia Jankovec and Annette Clay and Fay Harden and other dear friends there has emerged a portrait of Christine Jack, a portrait of a person whom you feel like you almost knew and understood and admired; a portrait of a wonderful, loving, caring mother, a mother who could never have abandoned her children, a mother who cannot be with Kairsten and Adam now because she is dead.

For a little while I would ask you to recall again with me some of the testimony concerning this lovely person.

Mrs. Jankovec met Christine's father and mother, Stephan and Veletei Reiter, at a Christmas party back in 1964. She has been a close family friend ever since.

To nine-year old Christine, she was Tante Lidijia.

Mrs. Jankovec described the child as a nice, bubbly little girl. She told you that she has been close to Christine for 24 years, that she hadn't changed very much, that she was happy and outgoing, full of zest and always laughing.

To Christine's children, Adam and Kairsten, Mrs. Jankovec was 'Baka,' grandmother, even though they were not actually related.

Aunt Lidijia, "Baka," mother and grandmother herself, whose daughter had children of her own, was asked to talk about Christine Jack the mother.

"Adam and Kairsten were always with their mother," she said. "They were very close. They would hang around her like little birds. She would always stop and help them and hug them like a good mother does. She was a very good mother."

Donna Mae Henry had many opportunities to assess Christine Jack the mother. Her daughter Lauren and Christine's daughter Kairsten were "pals," she said. "Kairsten was like my own daughter and Lauren was like a daughter to Chris."

Donna Henry said that as a mother, Christine was "a role model. Everything was for the children."

Cheryl MacMillan knew Christine since they were in grade ten together and both were 15 years old. They became very close friends, remained close while they were at university and even lived together for a while before they got married. Then Christine married Brian Jack and Cheryl married her husband David and they had their children at approximately the same time.

Cheryl became Auntie Cheryl to Adam and Kairsten.

You will remember how she described the manner in which Christine raised her children: "Chris was a wonderful mother to her children and she adored them. She would have done anything for them."

Fay Harden, Annette Clay and Reid Schindel expressed similar sentiments, as did so many others.

I say most respectfully to you, ladies and gentlemen, that it is open to you to conclude that only death could keep this loving mother apart from her children.

Appendix

Who was in a better position to corroborate, that is, to confirm the testimony of all of these witnesses as to the kind of mother Christine Jack was than Brian Jack himself?

While Constable Paquette was questioning the accused about Christine's disappearance, he asked him whether "this kind of action is in character with your wife."

Please remember Brian Jack's answer: "No, it's not. She's a caring mother and it just isn't like her to leave the kids behind."

And you will recall, as well, that he told Constables Kashuba and Pelland that he was sure that something had happened to Christine because she wouldn't have left without the kids.

So, many, many people attested to Christine's relationship with her children. David MacMillan described her as an exceptional parent. Kathryn Walz told you of how proud Chris was of her children.

The magnetic pull of a mother's love towards her children is a powerful force indeed.

It is a proven fact that Christine Jack has not been with her children since the early hours of Saturday night, December 17, 1988.

This proven fact, this separation of a mother and children, is the first vital link in a long chain of circumstantial evidence which I submit, coupled with other damning pieces of evidence, can lead to but one logical inference—that the fact of Christine Jack's death has been proven beyond all reasonable doubt.

Another specific element in the crime of murder which the Crown must prove is the identity of the accused; that is, the Crown must prove that the person charged with the murder is the one who actually committed it.

In this case, the circumstances pointing both to the murder of Christine Jack and to Brian Jack as the perpetrator are so interwoven, I suggest, that even though your deliberations fall into two successive stages, namely (a) the question as to whether Christine is dead; and (b) the question as to whether it was Brian who killed her, the whole of the evidence bears on both questions. Proof of the commission of the alleged murder is inextricably bound up with the proof of Brian Jack's connection with it.

It is for you, the ladies and gentlemen of the jury, to decide how much credence is to be given to Brian Jack's contention that on Saturday night, December 17, 1988, in the family room at 170 Alburg Drive, there was a discussion about marriage problems. And then "Chris got up, grabbed her winter coat and purse, got into the yellow Blazer and drove off."

How much credence are you prepared to give to Brian Jack's account of his wife's departure?

How much faith do you have in his story to police?

How much reliance are you prepared to place on Brian Jack's version of his wife's disappearance?

In order to answer these questions, it might be well to review some of the testimony of the witnesses with whom Brian spoke about Christine's departure.

Perhaps our review should start on Sunday, December 18, 1988.

At 10:46 p.m. Brian Jack telephoned the Winnipeg Police Missing Persons Bureau and reported that his wife of eight years, Christine Anna Jack, 33 years of age, had left the family home at 170 Alburg Drive around 9:00 p.m. on Saturday, December 17, 1988 and that she had not returned home.

He reported that there had been a domestic quarrel prior to his wife's departure, that she had left the family home and driven off in the yellow family 1983 Chevrolet Blazer, two-door, license plate number 482 DGK.

Now Constables Ronald Hoglund and Donald Gresson familiarized themselves with the content of the missing person's report. Then, at 1:09 a.m. on Monday, December 19, they arrived at the Jack residence on what they described as a normal missing person's follow-up.

Gresson stated that Hoglund asked Jack for any reason why his wife may have left the house, and Jack indicated that they did have some "discussions regarding financial problems, and, in particular, he said "there was a shortfall of cash."

The officer stated that "Mr. Jack appeared calm and gave intelligent answers to the questions put to him."

Constable Darlene Kashuba testified, you will remember, that she and her partner, Constable James Pelland, went over to 170 Alburg Drive on Tuesday, December 20, at approximately 11:15 in the morning, in connection with the report of the missing Christine Jack.

She told you that Mr. Jack appeared sick, quiet, dull, reserved, and showed no outward sign of emotion.

"He appeared to be suffering from a cold. That's my opinion," she said. "He answered the questions as we asked them, but he didn't offer too much."

Constable Kashuba advised you that she had briefed herself with the missing person's report and had found no major inconsistencies in the content of the report and what Mr. Jack had told her and Constable Pelland.

On cross-examination she acknowledged that Mr. Jack answered all the questions in a forthright manner.

Her estimated time with the accused was about a half hour.

Appendix

Constable Kashuba said:

> We began speaking to Brian Jack. He related to us that on Sunday evening his wife wanted to talk. She couldn't stand living with him any more and wanted him to leave. This led to a heated argument.

I pause at this point to remind you that Constable Kashuba was making notes of Brian Jack's comments and stated that she believed her notes to be accurate.

The constable continued:

> He then indicated that she had gotten hysterical and at approximately 9:30 that evening, she left in their truck. I understood this to be the yellow Blazer. He further related to us that at the time of her leaving, she had not taken any clothing with her. And he said that he was sure that something had happened to her because she wouldn't have left without the kids.

Jack told the two officers that as far as he was aware, Christine had no boyfriends.

Just incidentally, ladies and gentlemen, you may recall Mr. Kaplan having asked Constable Kashuba whether Mr. Jack had made any initial comment to her or to Constable Pelland, any inquiries of any nature. She replied, "No."

You may find it most unusual that when the two police officers attended upon Mr. Jack on that Tuesday morning, some 36 hours after he had reported his wife's disappearance, he hadn't anxiously blurted out "Have you any news about my wife? Has she been found?"

Nevertheless, Constable Pelland agreed that Jack gave the appearance of being concerned about his wife.

As to whether this concern was feigned or real, genuine or invented, that is for you to decide.

I have already alluded to the testimony of Constable Jay Paquette, who went to the Jack residence on Thursday morning, December 22, at about nine o'clock to ascertain from Mr. Jack whether he had received any information with regard to his missing wife.

Jack told the constable that Christine got up, grabbed her winter coat, got into the truck which he described as a 1983 Blazer, and drove off.

"I didn't know what to do and just waited around the house," the accused told the officer. "I thought maybe she went for a coffee or a drive to think things out. Then I made a pot of coffee and I was so upset that when I was in the family room, I spilled coffee on the cushion. I just waited and I guess I fell asleep. When I woke up, she hadn't come back. I waited a little longer, phoned a few people and called you guys."

One evening last week I was sitting in my den, ladies and gentlemen, pondering over what I was going to say to you in my closing address. I had just reviewed my notes on Constable Paquette's testimony. I came to the part where the accused spoke of spilling the coffee and falling asleep and awakening to find that Christine was not there.

And then I remembered those telling words of President Abraham Lincoln, a man who spoke to ordinary people like yourselves in ordinary, simple language: "You can fool all of the people some of the time and some of the people all of the time, but you can't fool all of the people all of the time."[27]

Brian Jack made some rather startling telephone calls, commencing at about five o'clock on Sunday morning, December 18, 1988.

He spoke to friends about Christine's departure.

He inquired of them as to her whereabouts.

He had now embarked upon his pathetically obvious, yet nonetheless diabolical, scheme to divert suspicion from himself.

But alas, poor Brian just couldn't keep his facts straight. He got all mixed up and he gave different versions to different people of the circumstances surrounding Christine's leaving. Why, he couldn't even be consistent about the time that she was supposed to have left the house and driven off in the Blazer.

He phoned David MacMillan at about five o'clock that Sunday morning and told him that Chris had left at about nine o'clock.

Peter Henry's phone rang at 5:30 a.m. and Jack told him that Chris had left somewhere between 9:30 and ten o'clock.

Incidentally, you will remember that he told Constables Kashuba and Pelland that she left at approximately 9:30 that evening.

Annette Clay testified that Brian called her at 5:45 a.m. and talked for 15 minutes. He said that Chris left between 10:00 and 11:00 p.m. I asked Mrs. Clay twice about the departure time between 10:00 and 11:00 p.m. and she was most adamant. You may recall that My Lord, the Chief Justice, questioned Mrs. Clay as well about the alleged time of departure. The witness did not recant: "Brian said she left between 10:00 and 11:00."

To recap:

At five a.m., he said that she had left about nine o'clock; at 5:30 a.m., he said that she had left between 9:30 and ten o'clock; and at 5:45 a.m., he said that she had left between ten and eleven o'clock.

You may find it most extraordinary, to say the least, these striking discrepancies in Jack's accounts of the time that Christine supposedly left the house.

And how did Brian Jack describe what happened in the family room just before Christine left?

He told David MacMillan that they had had a disagreement the night before.

He told Annette Clay that they had an argument and discussion as to where the marriage was going.

You may find it extraordinary then that in his telephone conversation with Mrs. Jankovec early Sunday morning, he told her that he and Chris had had a fight the night before and were screaming at each other.

On December 20, to Constables Kashuba and Pelland, he said it was a heated argument.

You may find it extraordinary that Brian Jack had his wife leaving the house anywhere from 9:00 p.m. to 11:00 p.m.

You may find it extraordinary that he changed the discussion from a disagreement to an argument and then to a fight in which they were screaming at each other, depending upon whom he was speaking with.

And then again, you may not find it extraordinary at all; that is, if you are satisfied that Christine Jack did not leave the house in the manner in which her husband said she did.

I think you will agree with me, ladies and gentlemen, that as the evidence unfolded, it became more and more apparent that Mr. Jack's credibility was becoming extremely questionable.

He told his outlandish story of Christine's disappearance to Constables Hoglund and Gresson, Kashuba and Pelland, and again to Constable Paquette. He told Peter and Donna Mae Henry. He told David and Cheryl MacMillan. He told Aunt Lidijia and David Knechtel and Reid Schindel. He told Kathryn Walz and Annette Clay. And he told many others as well.

He told everyone, everyone except Mrs. Reiter, Christine's mother, the one person he just couldn't bring himself to call with this preposterous story.

You may find it curious that Mrs. Reiter was not on Brian Jack's list.

And then again, you may not find it at all curious.

Do you believe that at about three o'clock on Sunday morning, December 18, Brian Jack knocked on Peter and Donna Mae Henry's door?

Let us examine the evidence.

David MacMillan testified that Brian Jack told him that Christine had left in the Blazer the evening before and that he had anticipated that she would only be gone for an hour; that he waited from nine o'clock until 5:00 a.m. and then called him.

Mr. MacMillan stated that Brian said that he had gone down to the Henrys'.

"I can't recall," he said, "whether Brian maintained during the five o'clock call that he went down to the Henrys', or whether he told me at the time of our discussions on the following Tuesday or Wednesday. I think it was during the early morning phone call that he said that. In any event, he said that he knocked on the Henrys' door at about three o'clock and got no response."

Donna Mae Henry went to bed between one o'clock and 1:30. She testified that she is a light sleeper and would have heard a knock at the door.

Brian Jack did not knock on the Henrys' door, ladies and gentlemen. Please recall Peter Henry's evidence in this connection.

He watched the whole of the second Gene Hackman movie.

The movie ended at 3:29, according to the VCR clock. He rewound the movie, followed his usual "little ritual," which took five to ten minutes, and was in bed around 3:45 a.m.

He described the layout of his home, a four-level split with an open floor plan. He watched the movie on the VCR located in the den, which is about 15 feet from the door at the front entrance.

He stated that there are five stairs leading from the entranceway up to the den, dining room and bedroom area and that the whole area is not divided by a wall.

He described the lighting conditions, both inside and outside the home, that existed while he was watching the movie: a light on in the den and a light on in the living room, which consisted of one single lamp located by a window facing onto the street. The Christmas tree lights were on, as were three outside lights, one next to the doorway and two on either side of the garage.

He told you that there is a vertical window, four feet by one foot, beside the door.

He also told you that because of the proximity of the television set to the master bedroom, he kept the volume as low as humanly possible so that there was very little chance that he would have missed hearing anything.

In answer to Mr. Kaplan's question to Mr. Henry, "Did any visitors come to your home or knock on your door or ring the bell?" the witness replied, "No one approached the home. No one rang the bell."

Looking back now, you may wonder why Mr. Wolson asked Mr. Henry whether Brian Jack wore a watch.

"He didn't wear a watch, to the best of my knowledge," Peter Henry replied.

"No doubt Brian Jack was wrong about the time at which he knocked on Mr. Henry's door," my learned friend is bound to say to you. I have no doubt he will tell you that even though Brian Jack said he knocked on the Henrys' door about three o'clock, Mr. Wolson will stress that the accused was really only guessing about the time, because he didn't have a watch. He really didn't know the time. And that he knocked on the door after Peter Henry had gone to sleep, some time after a quarter to four.

Mr. Wolson, I am confident, will stress the fact that Brian Jack didn't wear a watch.

And he will, I am certain, place equal emphasis on the fact that Mrs. Jankovec wears a hearing aid.

No doubt the skillful Mr. Wolson will argue that just as sleep prevented Peter Henry from hearing Brian Jack's knock on the door, impaired hearing prevented Aunt Lidijia from accurately hearing what Brian Jack said to her.

Peter Henry and Lidijia Jankovec have sharp ears, ladies and gentlemen.

I ask you to be very wary when Mr. Wolson talks to you about wristwatches and hearing aids.

Brian Jack expressed concern to Peter Henry about the Blazer overheating.

Why, you may ask, would he have brought up the subject of the mechanical condition of the vehicle, which he claimed his wife had left in during that 5:30 a.m. phone call to his neighbour, Peter Henry?

Jack related the fact that he had driven it the day before and he felt that there was something mechanically wrong with it. He said that the vehicle's heater would stop giving heat and the warning lights would come on.

I ask you to pause and reflect upon this for a moment.

Yes indeed, Brian Jack had driven the vehicle the day before. Or, more accurately, the night before, when he drove it out to Ste. Anne and beyond.

That is why he knew, firsthand, about the problem with the overheating.

Peter Henry testified that during the fairly short 8:30 Sunday morning telephone conversation, the accused elaborated on the subject of the Blazer overheating.

You may find it curious that Brian Jack appeared so concerned about the mechanical condition of the Blazer and the fact that it was overheating, so concerned that he mentioned it twice to Peter Henry on two separate occasions.

Then again, you may not find it curious at all.

The significance of these comments demonstrates how this expression of concern for his wife in a mechanically unsafe and freezing vehicle was calculated to divert, once again, any suspicion from himself when Christine failed to turn up.

Christine Jack was dead.

Brian Jack, that stranger to the truth, while giving the appearance of showing grave concern for his wife, never dreamed that his diabolical scheme would backfire in his face in what he may always regard as a cruel twist of fate.

Even Brian Jack, a man of both limited imagination and even more limited integrity, could never have dreamed that an overheating radiator would so disrupt his plan that it would detour him from his easterly flight on the Trans-Canada Highway and into the little village of Ste. Anne.

Even in his wildest dreams, he could never have anticipated this chance meeting with the good people of that community: Brenda Appleyard, Roger Pilloud, the Simards and Paul St. Marie, all of whom identified him as the tall stranger in their midst.

I say to you, ladies and gentlemen, that but for a boiling radiator, an act of God perhaps, it is extremely unlikely that we would be together today attending to our respective duties.

I will return to the subject of the "Ste. Anne Connection" a little further down the road.

Might I now ask that you explore with me Brian Jack's pathetic fairy tale concerning the spilled coffee?

You will remember David MacMillan having told you that he went over to the Jack residence on Tuesday, December 20. He wanted Brian to repeat what he had said on Sunday, everything from the moment that Christine left.

He said that on Wednesday, December 21, Brian dropped by his house, that Cheryl and the children were on their way out to a Christmas concert and, so, he and Brian had an impromptu supper, hot-dogs.

"Basically," Mr. MacMillan testified, "we had a similar type of conversation to that of Tuesday. The spilling of the coffee came up again. In recapping what had happened, this was the second time that he brought up the subject of the spilled coffee. I didn't think it particularly relevant," Mr.

MacMillan said, "and I didn't pursue it."

Well, ladies and gentlemen, from the Prosecution's standpoint, Brian Jack's reference to spilling the coffee is vitally relevant because once again it demonstrates clearly that there are times when his lies catch up with him. You see, it wasn't coffee that he spilled. What he spilled was his wife's blood.

No, he didn't try to remove coffee stains from the couch because there were none. What he tried so unsuccessfully to do was to obliterate the blood of his wife that was embedded in the cushion.

He tried to wash it out using Fleecy or Downy.

I would ask you to recall that Brian Jack laid this preposterous piece of fiction on Constable Paquette on Thursday, December 22:

> I thought maybe she went out for a coffee or for a drive to think things out. Then I made a pot of coffee and I was so upset when I was in the family room, I spilled coffee on the cushion,

The blood is still on the cushion, ladies and gentlemen. It just won't wash. It won't wash any more than any other of Brian Jack's lies.

Many witnesses participated in the painting of the portrait of Christine Jack. They portrayed her not only as a loving mother and warm and unselfish friend, but as well, as a person who, despite her matrimonial problems, was optimistic about tomorrow and was making future plans.

No matter what my learned friend may say to you about Christine's downer moods and mood swings, ladies and gentlemen, the evidence is overwhelmingly crystal clear: Christine Jack had every intention of going on living!

There isn't a shred of evidence that she was suicidal or clinically depressed or ever had been. Might we now consider some irrefutable assertions in this regard? We can even go back to the time when Christine was nine years old, "a nice, bubbly little girl," as Aunt Lidijia described her, "a person who hadn't changed much through the years, full of zest, laughing."

Mr. Wolson will no doubt remind you that although Mrs. Jankovec acknowledged on cross-examination that Christine was upbeat and happy in the eighties, in December of 1988 she was not happy any more and that there had been a change in her personality even before that.

He will, I am sure, go back to his cross-examination of Donna Mae Henry and refer to those days at the end of November of 1988, when Mrs. Henry said that "Chris would come over and she would be crying, very emotional and extremely upset."

He will insist that this normally "very upbeat person" had obviously changed dramatically over a three-week period.

Ladies and gentlemen, I suggest to you that Christine Jack's distress at that particular time was understandable. But it must be kept in its proper perspective despite what Mr. Wolson may ask you to conjure up to the contrary.

Please remember what Donna Mae Henry told you about Christine's appearance and mood the day before she disappeared.

It was Friday morning, December 16, 1988. Mrs. Henry was at work at the Health Sciences Centre. Christine dropped off some aerobic wear and arrangements were made to go shopping that evening.

"She looked really nice," Mrs. Henry said. "I remember she had just had her hair done the night before, and she had on her fur coat and I thought to myself how well she looked, because in the last two weeks she had lost weight and she was always tired and haggard looking.

"She seemed up, it was a better day than lately. She was happy, more like her old self."

Christine Jack had absolutely no intention whatsoever of throwing in the towel. There is all kinds of evidence which establishes, beyond all doubt, that she would carry on despite her turmoil over a shattered marriage.

Alfred Kircher, Christine's immediate supervisor at the Child Guidance Clinic since September of 1985, met with her, at her request, on Wednesday, September 14.

He spoke of those things Christine talked about, that she was going to leave Brian, that she had made a definite decision, that she was consulting Dr. McPhee to get help, more for Brian than for herself.

Mr. Kircher, who is a psychologist, did not find her to be clinically depressed. He met with her just three days before her disappearance.

He was asked, "What impression did she leave with you at the conclusion of the conversation insofar as her future was concerned and the direction in which her life was headed?"

He replied, "At the end of the half-hour session, she went off as if she had a lot of plans for the future, and was optimistic."

Christine went Christmas shopping with Donna Henry on December 16. Christmas was only nine days away. She was preparing for the festive season.

You will remember that the two ladies went for a bite to eat after their shopping expedition. It was at Schmecker's Restaurant that Chris gave Donna $400 to put in a bank account for her, a little nest egg if she and Brian separated.

Donna told you that Chris said that she was going to wait until mid-January and then she would get a court order to get him out of the house at that time.

I don't propose to go over everything that was said in this conversation. Collectively, you will recall all of it.

I would just remind you that Christine said that if she sold the house, she would stay in St. Vital and would remain close to Donna so that their daughters, Kairsten and Lauren, would be together.

Ladies and gentlemen, on Friday night, December 16, 1988, just about 24 hours before her disappearance, Christine seemed happy. She was making future plans.

On Saturday, December 17, at five o'clock, Cheryl MacMillan phoned her. They couldn't talk about a lot of things because Brian was there. They chatted for an estimated ten minutes.

Among other things, they discussed the dinner which was to be held at Cheryl's house the following Monday night.

During their brief conversation, they talked about what Donna and Chris would bring—a Greek salad and a dessert, if my memory serves me.

"Chris seemed really happy," Cheryl MacMillan said. "She was looking forward to the dinner and seemed much happier."

On Saturday, December 17, at about 9:50 in the morning, Donna and Christine had a brief telephone conversation. Donna said, as you will recall, that Chris was in a really good mood. "Chris was going to take Kairsten to a ringette game early Sunday morning."

And then Donna Henry testified that it was about twenty to eight that Saturday evening, just after she got back from her sister's, that she phoned Christine, just to see how her day had gone and to make arrangements for the following day: "She was still in a good mood. I didn't find her to be really that different from the morning. She wasn't distraught."

This was the last time, just a couple of hours before her friend vanished, that Donna Mae Henry would ever talk with Christine Jack.

It is open to you, ladies and gentlemen, to find as a fact that Christine Jack was planning for her own future and that of her children on Saturday evening, December 17, 1988, right up until the moment when her life was so needlessly snuffed out.

If further evidence were required to reveal Christine Jack's state of mind and emotional health just before her death, it can readily be ascertained from the letter she wrote to her mother and father on December 16, 1988, a letter which she didn't get around to mailing.

When you finally begin deliberating on your verdict, I respectfully ask you to study Exhibit 101, this letter, very, very carefully.

There are just one or two sentences that I would emphasize, if I may.

In the second paragraph, Christine wrote: "I'm finding out that I have more strength and determination than I realized." Christine Jack obviously was not a quitter.

"I know my decision to leave Brian is the best one for me and I think in the long run it will be better for the children to live in a more peaceful and happier environment."

Here we see clearly how logically and rationally she was thinking and planning. Hardly the words of a defeated, confused, depressed woman, I respectfully suggest.

In the middle of page two, you will read:

My next step is to get Brian to move out, hopefully in January. He said he can't move out until we sell the house, because he needs money. However, according to Jan (the lawyer), I don't have to sell the house and he will have to leave, either of his own free will or by a court order. I would rather he leave on his own, but I'm not sure that he will. The next few weeks will still be tough.

Witness after witness attested as to Christine Jack's many sterling qualities: her devotion to her children, her loyalty to her friends, her strength in her adversity, her aspirations for the future.

Another shining quality of hers is her selflessness, her compassion for her husband and his well-being even though, as far as she was concerned, the marriage was over. Her insistence on his seeing Dr. McPhee, her concern over his emotional health, even though she had decided that soon they would go their separate ways, is further evidence that this compassionate lady wanted to let her husband down easily.

Now, as to the accused's state of mind in the latter part of November and throughout December of 1988, ladies and gentlemen, might we examine the evidence in this connection?

I suggest as a starting point that we consider the undated letter that Brian Jack wrote to Christine's father, Stephan Reiter, and which he received in late November:

Steve, I am writing you this letter because I am at my wit's end. I would like some advice from you in order to save our marriage. Christine means everything to me.

I love her more than anything in the world. We are both seeing a priest this week and we are going to a marriage counsellor on Friday, the 9th of December, at 3:15 p.m. I will try anything in order to get a chance to make it work. I have no one here to talk to and Chris refuses to discuss anything with me beyond saying that she has no feeling left for me."

He goes on to write about how she had loved him very much, but it was now as if she were a different person.

You will note his comment that "it is not fair to anyone."

He wrote: "My love for Christine can overcome any obstacles."

I would ask you to give particular attention to the line which follows:

"I'm being very patient and am not putting pressure on her."

He concluded the letter:

"I'll be waiting for your letter or phone call. I don't have anybody else to turn to."

Mr. Reiter did not respond to this letter.

One of the elements in the charge of murder which the Crown must prove is the intention to kill. What is in the mind of the accused at the time of the killing is of paramount importance.

What motivates a person to commit murder is also of vital significance. His thoughts and words preceding the homicide can be very significant.

Throughout the testimony of Kathryn Walz, as well, you were able, I am sure, to get a very accurate account of Brian Jack's thoughts and feelings in late 1988 and, more particularly, on December 15, just two days before this tragedy occurred.

I propose to review Mrs. Walz's evidence in some detail because I believe it will assist you greatly in determining the state of mind of the accused at this crucial time.

Mrs. Walz, you will recall, is a school psychologist who was at Fort Rouge School on Thursday, December 15, when at eleven o'clock that morning, she was summoned to the principal's office, where she received a telephone call from Brian Jack which lasted for about half an hour.

Mrs. Walz was amazed at receiving this call in that the caller had had to track her down through her secretary and, further, because she had never spoken to Brian Jack on the telephone before. She was certainly surprised that he had called her at work.

He identified himself and then he started to talk about the fact that he and Chris were having some problems. He talked about them being separated, but not really separated in that they were living in the same house. He commented on their deteriorating relationship and advised Mrs. Walz that they had been going for some marriage counselling and that he wanted to save his marriage.

He said that he didn't feel good about the counselling; that it made him feel small, it made him feel insignificant, it made him feel like dirt.

Mrs. Walz stated that she took notes at the start of the conversation. She noted that Brian Jack said that he had forced himself on Christine sexually.

He said he had done things that he shouldn't have done and knew he shouldn't have.

He then went on to tell her that things had been difficult for him over the last few years. He talked about his problems with the Fit Stop and his business and he said that he worried all the time.

He said something about having been married before and that when he met Chris, he expected that this time it would be for life.

Mrs. Walz said he sounded calm and normal. What was abnormal, however, was the fact that Brian Jack had called her in the first place.

You may reflect upon the fact that Kathryn Walz was not a close, intimate friend. You may ponder as to why he told her that Chris was his "strength," his "rock" and that he wanted "things to be right, things to be forever."

Out of Brian Jack's own mouth, ladies and gentlemen, through his words and by his own actions a very clear and detailed picture of the accused has emerged.

And this picture, if you examine it carefully, is not the picture of the mild, non-aggressive, former football player that Mr. Wolson tried to paint, a gentle, almost Ghandi-like pacifist.

Annette Clay, a loyal friend, told you that "Brian is always a nice guy. His nickname is Bugs. He's very gentle, a teddy bear," she said.

Mr. Wolson will argue strenuously, I am certain, that this quiet, concerned, non-aggressive, loving husband could never have harmed Christine if his life depended on it.

Don't be deceived, ladies and gentlemen. Brian Jack is not always a nice guy. Sometimes he is not so gentle either.

He had so terrified his wife that at one point she was concerned for her life.

It was on the night of December 9 or 10, Donna Mae Henry testified, that Chris was at her house:

> She sat on the corner of my bed. She was crying and she was very upset and she said to me, "If anything happens to me, Donna, will you take care of the kids for me?"

Mrs. Henry stated that Christine was terrified and didn't know whether to wait or to move out.

She also told you that Christine called her at work and was very upset about what Brian had done to her the night before, that is, Thursday, December 8. She said that he had pinned her down on the bed for five or ten minutes, that she had been terrified and was crying and that he had made her promise that she wouldn't leave until he could get a job. She said that she didn't sleep at all that night and didn't know where to turn or what to do.

Mrs. Jankovec remembered that Christine had called her from work, that she was crying and that she had said, "Brian threw me on the bed and pinned me down and said that I wasn't listening to him."

"If it's so bad, pack your bags and bring the kids over," Mrs. Jankovec told you she suggested to Christine.

Christine, she testified, said no because there was to be a meeting with a marriage counsellor the next day and she wanted to give Brian another chance.

Mr. Peter Henry sheds some light on one facet of Brian Jack's personality—his latent anger. I will touch on it, as you may find it rather significant.

During the latter part of November, he invited Jack to the Carlton Club primarily so that "Brian would have someone to talk to about his marital situation," he said.

Mr. Henry testified that "the conversation centered around the idea that Brian was very confused about what was happening in his life with regard to his marriage. He felt that he was dedicated to Chris and the children and the marriage and he was upset and dismayed over what was happening."

"His mood, to me, was one of anger because this was happening and he couldn't fully understand why," Peter Henry said. "Upset and dismayed, pretty well describe what I observed.

"He told me," Mr. Henry continued, "that he had committed himself to the reconciliation of the marriage and that he was doing what he could to turn things around. He was getting help from the religious field, a priest, I think. He felt that he was getting something solid by way of a job."

Peter Henry was with Brian Jack on Friday evening, December 16, while his wife Donna and Christine Jack were Christmas shopping. The fathers took the children to a Christmas performance in the Exchange District.

If you bear in mind that they were together just 24 hours prior to Christine's final journey, it will be helpful to recall what Mr. Henry said about the accused's mood that evening.

In answer to Mr. Kaplan's question, "What was your impression of his demeanour and attitude on December 16th?" Mr. Henry replied:

> Brian turned to me and said that he was really disappointed that the whole family was not together. He seemed upset and somewhat angry that his wife Christine wasn't there.

Yes, there was a darker side to the gentle, non-aggressive Brian Jack that his friend Annette Clay never saw.

There was an anger which had been smoldering and building since the end of November.

Finally, ladies and gentlemen, it was beginning to dawn on Brian Jack that his marriage to Christine was over.

The counselling, he realized, made him feel insignificant. He was quickly losing his self-esteem. The counselling, he said, made him feel like dirt.

That Brian Jack loved his wife dearly, there can be no question.

She was his strength, his rock.

Life without Christine would be no life for him, he had told Aunt Lidijia.

But there came a time when Christine could no longer stand the sight of him.

At last, he came to realize this and he couldn't endure it.

Christine could live without him.

She told him to leave.

That was the straw that, in truth, broke the camel's back.

And in his anger, he lashed out at her and her heart stopped beating forever.

❖ ❖ ❖ ❖ ❖

Ladies and gentlemen of the jury:

Brian Jack lied to the police and to his friends and acquaintances when he told them about Christine's departure.

Appendix

Christine Jack did not drive away from 170 Alburg Drive in the yellow Blazer on Saturday night, December 17, 1988, some time between nine and 11:00 p.m.

No, ladies and gentlemen, that is not at all what happened.

It was Brian Jack who drove off in the Blazer shortly after 9:00 p.m.

And it is open to you, having regard to all of the evidence you have heard in this case, to draw the logical inference that the body of Christine Jack was in the back of the Blazer as the accused drove away.

I concede that there is no evidence before the court as to what he intended to do with the body.

So, too, there is no evidence as to how or where he disposed of it.

But this we do know: That his disposal plan was interrupted because of a leaking radiator hose and he unexpectedly found himself in the Village of Ste. Anne shortly after 10:00 p.m.

Constable Munroe told you that Ste. Anne is about 25 miles southeast of Winnipeg.

Lie as he might about not having left his home that Saturday night, Brian Jack did, in fact, leave home.

Between 10:10 and 10:15 p.m. he walked into the Ste. Anne Hotel.

I know that you will remember Brenda Louise Appleyard's testimony in this connection.

Miss Appleyard is Mr. Roger Pilloud's housekeeper. He owns the Ste. Anne Hotel. She has been a bartender at the hotel for the past three years. She also books the bands that play at the hotel.

She had booked the Ken-D Band to offer its musical stylings in the hotel beverage room on Friday night, December 16, and Saturday night, December 17, 1988.

We were told that the boys in the band drew a much smaller crowd on Saturday night, the seventeenth, about a quarter of the number of patrons they had played to the night before.

Apparently these rascals were supposed to start playing at 8:30 but they didn't show up until after nine, we were told.

Perhaps a little levity now and again, to break the tension during a murder trial, doesn't hurt.

Reference was not made to the antics of these unruly musicians, however, just to generate a bit of laughter.

Brenda Appleyard elaborated on her dealings with the Ken-D Band in order to explain why she was able to pinpoint the exact year, month, day, hour and almost the precise minute that the tall stranger spoke to her in the bar.

Miss Appleyard testified that the band had started playing again at ten o'clock. She said, "It could have been the second song of their second set, which would have been close to 10:10 or 10:15."

She continued:

> He came up to the bar and asked if there was a garage or gas station open. I told him, "Not at this time of night." I asked him what the problem was and he said he had trouble with his truck, that it had broken down.

Miss Appleyard was at the bar with the stranger for no more than five minutes, perhaps less, and two feet away from him in lighting conditions which she compared to the illumination in this courtroom. "The lighting in the bar," she said, "has half the intensity of the lighting in this place."

Miss Appleyard, like the other Ste. Anne witnesses, was examined and cross-examined as to how the tall stranger was dressed, his approximate height, weight, build, size, facial hair, moustache, eye colour, skin colour and even his racial origin. I don't propose to review all of these observations with you. Collectively, you will recall the testimony of each of the witnesses insofar as the identification of the stranger is concerned.

But let me say this: In this very courtroom Miss Appleyard pointed to, and identified, Brian Jack as being the person who walked into the Ste. Anne Hotel between 10:10 and 10:15 on Saturday night, December 17, 1988.

Mr. Kaplan asked Miss Appleyard, "Are you identifying Mr. Jack, the person you see today, from the TV accounts?"

Her answer was a terse, "No."

Then you will remember that Sergeant Harry Williams testified that on the afternoon of December 29, he and Constable Creighton went to the Ste. Anne Hotel at 103 Dawson Road, where they showed Miss Appleyard a photopac of ten black and white photographs, which included a photograph of the accused. The accused's photograph was the fifth one in the pac.

Miss Appleyard was asked to go through the photos to see if the person who had been in the hotel was, in fact, in the photographs. She was told that there was a possibility that the person would not be there. She was asked to look at each picture carefully.

Sergeant Williams stated that on reaching photo number five, Miss Appleyard held up the picture and said, "This is him for sure."

Mr. Pilloud was shown the same photopac. Brian Jack's photograph

Appendix

was third in the pile this time.

Sergeant Williams testified that "Mr. Pilloud was asked to look at each picture carefully, which he did, and when he came to the third photo, he stated, 'I think this is the guy, but I'd know him for sure if I saw him.'"

During this trial, specifically on Wednesday, October 17, Mr. Pilloud unhesitatingly identified the accused.

You may not find this at all surprising. After all, Mr. Pilloud told you that he first saw the male individual when he walked into the bar.

"I watched him all the time he was there," said Mr. Pilloud. "I had nothing else to do."

The friendly hotel keeper said, you will remember, that the stranger was four feet away from him when they sat in the bar area and talked.

After the telephone call to Jim Hudrick, Mr. Pilloud sat at a table for 15 minutes with the man he identified in this courtroom as Brian Jack.

Murielle Simard also identified the accused. Might we consider her testimony for a minute or two?

She and her husband, Patrick, arrived at the hotel after the band had started playing. She told you that Patrick wanted to pick up a case of beer and, also, to hear the band.

This most observant witness described the stranger in this fashion:

He was very tall, over six feet, two inches. He weighed over 200 pounds. He had a toque on his head.

Mrs. Simard was within 15 feet of the man. She described the colour of his moustache as "not light, not dark."

She said the stranger was there for 20 minutes to half an hour, that the group at the table had talked about him because they had never seen him in Ste. Anne before and he had looked cold.

On two separate occasions, Mrs. Simard mentioned the accused's eyes, particularly as they were what she most remembered about him.

She, too, identified Brian Jack in this courtroom on Wednesday, October 17 as being the man she saw in the Ste. Anne Hotel on December 17, 1988.

She pointed to the accused and said, "He's sitting in the box. He doesn't look different, except he had on different clothes and he wore a toque."

I would ask you to recall something Mr. Wolson asked Mrs. Simard on cross-examination, "You never mentioned anything about his eyes in your statement to police, did you?" "No," she replied, "but I did see that his eyes were blue. I did say the colour of his eyes were blue because that's the thing I noticed most."

Trials & Errors: The People vs. Brian Gordon Jack

On the evening of January 12, 1989, Sergeant Williams and Sergeant Ryland went to the home of Mr. and Mrs. Patrick Simard with a different photopac consisting of ten coloured photographs. The officers spoke with Mr. and Mrs. Simard separately. Brian Jack's photograph was the fifth in the stack when Mrs. Simard viewed it.

This is what Sergeant Williams said to you:

> She viewed the picture pack, looking carefully at each photo until she reached number five. She said, "This is him. I saw the pictures in the newspaper but I wouldn't have recognized him from those. But I know him for sure by this photo. It looks exactly like him that night but he was wearing a toque."

In re-examination, Mrs. Simard clarified a point. She said, "I first saw his picture on TV. He was much younger then. But I recognized the shape of his face and mostly the eyes."

This may be as appropriate a time as any, ladies and gentlemen, to make a very brief comment about the evidence of the Charter House witnesses, Shirley Garbutt and Donna Pike. They, as you well realize, were called to the witness stand by the Bench and not by the Prosecution.

I don't propose to refer to their testimony. They appeared before you late last week and their words are fresh in your minds.

But I want to say this to you: The witnesses from Ste. Anne are honest and concerned citizens, ladies and gentlemen. The witnesses from the Charter House are honest but mistaken.

The reason that we do not ascribe 'concern' to Mrs. Garbutt and Mrs. Pike is self-evident. Seven days to report the alleged sighting and then Mrs. Garbutt's job was done. Never a further attempt to alert anyone!

Mrs. Pike called the next day. But never again an attempt by her to contact anyone, this with the full knowledge that Christine Jack was the mother of two young children; that police, helicopters and tracking dogs were combing the area around Ste. Anne. This, together with the fact that she knew that Brian Jack had been charged with murder, must make her alleged sighting suspect in your minds.

Honest, but mistaken.

You will hear a great deal about the alleged sightings from Mr. Wolson.

And it is inevitable as the flowers in May that he will have much to say about the failure of the Crown and the police to let him know about these alleged sightings with reasonable dispatch.

His voice will become louder, and his pitch higher, when he goes after

Appendix

the police. One way or another, he will castigate them for a shoddy investigation.

He will, I expect, tell you that had the police been more vigilant, no charges would have been laid because Christine would be found alive somewhere. He will use the proverbial double-edged sword.

But this fails to take into account the totality of the circumstantial evidence enveloping the accused in a tangled web of deceit and falsehood.

This sword cuts both ways. Had the police followed every lead and alleged sighting and continued to do so, I'm sure Mr. Wolson would then suggest to you that even the police were not satisfied beyond a reasonable doubt that Christine was dead.

Let me return now to the Ste. Anne connection.

Perhaps it would be helpful to briefly review Mr. Patrick Simard's testimony.

He told you that he had been at work before he and his wife, Murielle, went to the Ste. Anne Hotel. They arrived around 10:30 and sat at a table with his brother-in-law, Gilbert Gregoire. He recalled that Roger Pilloud joined them at their table and bought a round of drinks. Mr. Simard even remembered that he had had a 'Blue.'

I know that My Lord will give you some instructions as to identification evidence. He no doubt will speak about a witness's powers of observation.

I know, too, that you will cautiously evaluate the detailed testimony of the eagle-eyed witnesses Pilloud, Appleyard and the two Simards in this regard.

The astute Mr. Patrick Simard recalls that he had three beers at most, left around midnight, and that the members of the band were under the influence and that they were just not very good.

Consider, if you will, Mr. Simard's comments concerning this alien.

He was well dressed for the weather.

He went to the bar and talked to Brenda Appleyard for five to ten minutes, then he went and sat at a table by himself.

Roger Pilloud went over and sat with him for about half an hour.

This witness assured you that he got a good look at the stranger.

He was between six feet, three inches and six feet, five inches.

He weighed about 200 pounds. A fairly large individual.

He had a "light brown, blondish moustache, lighter as opposed to darker."

Mr. Simard, you will remember, stated that the stranger moved the dark toque back on his head, which revealed a receding hair line.

As to his age, Mr. Simard estimated him to be between 42 and 45 and said that he looked very inquisitive and that his eyes were shifting around as if he were looking for help.

On Thursday, October 18, Mr. Simard identified the accused Brian Jack as the stranger at the Ste. Anne Hotel.

When asked to make a comparison between the prisoner's present appearance and that of December 17, 1988, he said, "He looks the same, but he appears to have lost some weight."

Mr. Simard testified that he received a visit from Sergeant Williams and his partner on January 12, 1989. He said that he went through the photos that were handed to him in a stack by the sergeant and he picked one out.

"I asked the sergeant if this was the guy they were looking for," Mr. Simard said. "The officer didn't reply but he wrote my name on the back of the photograph," the witness told you.

You will remember that this witness also told you that the photo he chose was the photo of the person who was in the hotel bar that night.

I would ask you now to recollect Sergeant Williams' testimony in connection with Mr. Simard's identification of Brian Jack.

The sergeant testified that Mr. Jack's photo was number nine in order in the photopac. He said:

> Mr. Simard went through the picture pack, looking at each picture carefully. He reached number nine and put it aside. He looked at the final photo. He stated, "That's him," holding up number nine. "This is the guy. He's really tall, maybe six feet, four inches to six-foot-five. Really tall."

Sergeant Williams continued:

> I asked him, "Are you sure of your identification or have you identified him from pictures you have seen in the press or news media?" And Mr. Simard answered, "No, that's him for sure; no doubt about it."
>
> And the reason I asked that question, was because Brian Jack's picture had been on television.

And then you will remember Mr. Kaplan asking Mr. Simard this question: "Mr. Wolson spoke to you yesterday?"

"Yes," he replied. "He asked me if I could identify Brian Jack. He asked me if I was 25 percent, 50 percent sure; 75 percent or 100 percent sure. I

Appendix

said, 'I'm a 100 percent sure.'"

When you retire to consider your verdict, you will have the opportunity to examine the photographs in the two photopacs, both the black and white and the coloured. I know that you will study them carefully.

James Hudrick did not identify the accused.

"I was more concerned with the vehicle than the guy," he said.

However, this should present no difficulty for you, I respectfully suggest.

Mr. Hudrick went to the hotel, and Roger Pilloud pointed to a person seated at a table. This person left the hotel with Mr. Hudrick and showed him the vehicle and said something about it heating up and that a rad hose was perhaps busted.

Paul St. Marie, Jim Hudrick's brother-in-law, positively identified Brian Jack in this trial on Tuesday morning, October 23, as being the person whose Blazer he and Jim Hudrick had towed to Jim's garage from the Ste. Anne Hotel late Saturday night, December 17, 1988.

Paul said he saw the man's face under fluorescent lighting in Jim's garage.

"We had some conversation," Paul told you. They were at the garage, he estimated, for about half an hour.

He well remembered being in the detective office at the Public Safety Building on December 28, 1988 with Sergeant Williams and Constable Creighton. Why, he even remembered his exact words when he picked Brian Jack's photograph out of the photopac.

He told you that the sergeant said to him, "See if you recognize anyone."

He recognized the photographs of two people, one being a fellow by the name of Jim.

When he showed the officers Brian Jack's photograph, he said, "'That's the dude."

Sergeant Williams confirmed this.

He testified that both Hudrick and St. Marie were taken to the second floor detective office. St. Marie was placed in interview room number one and Hudrick in interview room number two.

The sergeant said:

After completing our interview with Mr. Hudrick, we entered interview room number one and spoke to Mr. Paul St. Marie. I showed him the photopac, and advised him that the person may be in this photopac and to look at it carefully. And he went through the photos.

On reaching photo four, that of Mr. Brian Jack, he threw it on the table towards us and stated, 'That's the dude!'

I asked him to continue going through the photopac and I made no suggestion that, in fact, that was the suspect. And on completing the viewing, he said that he was a hundred percent sure.

The sergeant, you will recall, told you that Paul continued through the pack and when he reached the photo of Mr. James Camrie, he said, "I know this fellow," and that he had been out in Ste. Anne.

"I believe it was a year prior to this," Paul St. Marie said, "that I saw him in the hotel there."

Inevitably, ladies and gentlemen, there would be minor discrepancies in the testimony of these various witnesses, and Mr. Wolson skillfully drew them to your attention.

But these discrepancies, I suggest, are of no moment. For example, on cross-examination, Mr. Wolson said to Paul St. Marie, "If somebody said you went into the hotel with Jim, they'd be wrong, wouldn't they?"

What is important, significant and uncontradicted is the fact that Paul identified Brian Jack as being the person who came out of the hotel with Jim Hudrick and took him over to the yellow Blazer with the overheating radiator.

Brenda Appleyard, Roger Pilloud, Patrick and Murielle Simard and Paul St. Marie all identified Brian Jack as having been in Ste. Anne, Manitoba shortly after ten minutes past ten o'clock on Saturday night, December 17, 1988.

These witnesses were resolute in their positive identification of the accused despite exhaustive cross-examination.

Yes, ladies and gentlemen, Brian Jack was in Ste. Anne that Saturday night.

He did not stay put at 170 Alburg Drive despite the fact that he told so many people that he was at home all night, waiting for Chris to return.

As I said before, there were times when Brian Jack was a stranger to the truth; there were times when he was a barefaced liar. This was one of those times.

The evidence establishes beyond a shadow of a doubt that he drove the Blazer into Ste. Anne on the night in question.

The evidence in support of the identification of the Jack Blazer in the village is just as positive and just as compelling as the identification of the accused himself, I respectfully suggest to you.

Appendix

You listened attentively to Paul St. Marie's testimony just a little while ago and it is fresh in your minds, I know, so I will not go over it too extensively.

You will recall his description of the vehicle. He said it was a yellow Blazer with factory rally wheels. Paul noticed the wheels because he would have liked to have had a set like those on his little S-10 truck. He observed a square tow hitch, the stripes along the sides and the spoiler on top of the back window. He recalled that the back windows were tinted as were the two side windows, and he remembered that the first letter in the license plate was D.

Mr. Kaplan then asked this witness to familiarize himself with photographs of the vehicle in Exhibit 1A (the booklet of photographs).

He referred to photographs 59, 60, 61 and 62. You might wish to refer to these photographs yourselves.

"This is the same Blazer," Paul St. Marie told you resolutely.

He studied photographs 63 and 64 and pointed to the scratch marks on the side of the housing which were made by the hooks during the towing.

He checked photographs 59 and 60 and referred to two clean spots.

"Our apron was up against it," he said.

In commenting on the square tow hitch that can be seen in photographs 59 and 60, the witness said, "That's the hitch. I never saw one like that before."

There was further evidence with respect to the identification of the Blazer.

Sergeant Williams testified that he and Constable Creighton met James Hudrick and Paul St. Marie on Wednesday morning, December 28.

They had rendezvoused at the Public Safety Building for the purpose of determining whether the suspect vehicle could be identified.

Sergeant Williams, you will recall, told you that he took Mr. Hudrick into the police garage to see if he could pick out the vehicle that he and young St. Marie had towed on December 17. Mr. Hudrick went directly to the suspect vehicle bearing plate number 482 DGK.

He observed that this vehicle had the same trailer hitch. He referred to the air spoiler above the rear window. He alluded to marks on the bumper made by the tow apron from the tow truck.

The sergeant said that Mr. Hudrick lifted the hood and noted that it was the same vehicle because of the antifreeze spray mixed with oil.

Just a word about this mixture of oil and antifreeze.

Mr. Wayne Greenlay, the civilian member of the Chemistry Section of the Crime Detection Laboratory, testified that he examined Exhibit 3, an oil sample taken from the fire wall of the Blazer, which can be seen in Exhibit 1A, photograph 56.

He examined, as well, Exhibit 74, a small jar containing antifreeze from the Blazer, and Exhibit 75, antifreeze taken from the Hudrick garage.

On the basis of instrumental and chemical examinations, he concluded, as did Mr. Hudrick, the mechanic, that because of the particular problems with the vehicle, there was this emulsified mixture of ethylene glycol, which is antifreeze and motor oil.

Jim Hudrick told Sergeant Williams that there was no doubt but that this was the vehicle.

Constable Creighton informed you that he had recorded that Paul St. Marie viewed the vehicle from 8:38 to 8:41, separately from Jim Hudrick, so that there weren't two witnesses viewing the same vehicle together.

The constable testified that Paul seemed excited and that he crawled under the Blazer with a flashlight.

"He positively identified it as the vehicle he had seen at Ste. Anne," Constable Creighton said. "I recorded Mr. St. Marie positively identifying this vehicle by a square trailer hitch and also by the letter D, which he indicated was the first letter on the plate.

Mr. St. Marie had also requested my flashlight," the officer continued, "which I lent him, and he then crawled underneath the vehicle and indicated that he had found strap marks from the tow truck sling. I also noted his reference to the metal air deflector, racing stripes, marks on the bumper and the canary-yellow colour."

The evidence that Brian Jack and the Jack family Blazer were in Ste. Anne, Manitoba shortly before ten o'clock on that Saturday night in December has been proven beyond any doubt whatsoever, I respectfully submit.

Hudrick's garage, to which the Jack vehicle was towed, is shown in photograph 67.

"I think Jim opened the garage doors," Paul said. "There was room to drive the whole Blazer into the garage. The tall fellow said that he would drive it in but the whole Blazer wasn't in the garage, just the front end," Jim Hudrick stated most emphatically.

The very precise St. Marie confirmed this. He said that the stranger drove only the front half of the vehicle into the garage.

The garage, you heard from both mechanics, was well lit with fluorescent lighting.

You may find it most extraordinary that Brian Jack drove only the front end of the Blazer into that well-lit garage on such a cold winter night in December.

And then again, there may be a logical inference for you to draw as to why he didn't want to drive it all the way in.

Now, Mr. Wolson may try to persuade you that Brian Jack didn't want to drive all the way into the garage and have the doors closed while the motor was running because of the exhaust fumes. He may try to convince you that this is common practice because a woman hadn't driven all the way into the Hudrick garage on another winter's day. Or he may try to urge upon you that the tractor was in the garage and blocking the Blazer's path.

It is open to you, ladies and gentlemen, to find as a fact that Brian Jack didn't want Paul St. Marie inside his vehicle, popping the hood.

It is open to you as well, I suggest, to conclude that Brian Jack did all he could to ensure that neither Hudrick nor St. Marie would get a good look into the Blazer through the front untinted windows.

Just incidentally, ladies and gentlemen, you will remember young Paul telling you that after he and Jim hooked up the Blazer, Jim drove the tow truck from the Ste. Anne Hotel lot out to his garage.

"Jim was driving," he said, "and this big guy sat on the right-hand side. I was in the middle. It was at that time that he said he had to get to Kenora that night. And then the guy mentioned having to get to Kenora that night again while we were over at Jim's garage."

Paul St. Marie shared with you his diagnosis of the Blazer's problem—a blown gasket or a cracked or warped head. He said:

> What happens, the antifreeze goes into the oil, into the oil jacket. Eventually what happens, it will seize the motor. We told him what was wrong with it and we offered to give him a ride back to the city.
>
> Well, he had to get to Kenora that night. He had to be there, the guy said.
>
> We would have given him a ride into the city, as I said, but we sure weren't going to drive him all the way to Kenora.

Jim Hudrick confirmed this reference to Kenora:

> He said he had to get to Kenora tonight. I told him he could leave his vehicle at my place and I would drive him to where he wanted to go.

Brian Jack talked about Kenora quite a bit that Saturday night.

Patrick Simard recalled that the stranger was asking how far it was from Ste. Anne to Kenora and that he was advised that it was about 100 miles.

In his cross-examination of Jim Hudrick, Mr. Wolson had this witness acknowledge that the Blazer needed work done on it, that it might seize up completely, and that he saw smoke coming from the back of the vehicle.

Mr. Wolson also suggested to Mr. Hudrick that the stranger had to get to a place where he could get certain kinds of parts.

Has Mr. Wolson raised a reasonable doubt in your minds, ladies and gentlemen, as to why Brian Jack was driving easterly down the Trans-Canada Highway close to midnight on that Saturday night?

Do you really believe he was off to Kenora to get new parts for his Blazer?

Might I digress for a moment.

At the end of his cross-examination of Constable Creighton, Mr. Wolson said to the officer, "It's good police work to get a lead and to follow it up, isn't it?"

The constable agreed.

And then Mr. Wolson said to the officer, "A lead can take you on a wild goose chase sometimes, can't it?"

The constable agreed again.

Mr. Wolson is very knowledgeable about wild goose chases, ladies and gentlemen. He has tried to take you on more than one of them himself during the course of this trial.

Brenda Appleyard testified that the accused told her he had to get to Kenora that night to pick up a truck. Roger Pilloud testified that the accused told him that he had to be in Kenora as he had to switch drivers, that he was supposed to meet the guy.

It is for you to decide whether Brian Jack spoke the truth when he said he had to pick up a truck in Kenora.

You may decide that Brian Jack lied to Mr. Pilloud about switching drivers, just as you may find that he lied to police about knocking on Peter Henry's door.

If I remember correctly, Jack told David MacMillan, too, about knocking on the Henry door.

Mr. Justice McInnes said that a criminal trial is a solemn inquiry into the truth. During this long and, at times, not too solemn inquiry into the truth, again and again Brian Jack's credibility—that is his capacity to speak the truth—has been found wanting.

Putting it more bluntly, the evidence reveals, I suggest, that the accused lied consistently to the police, to friends and to strangers in order to avoid detection as his wife's murderer and the one who subsequently disposed of her body.

Brenda Appleyard said the stranger was in a rush.

Roger Pilloud said that he appeared nervous and was moving in his chair all the time.

He was indeed in a rush. The sooner he could get out of Ste. Anne and on his way, the less likelihood someone might peer into the back of the Blazer.

Under ordinary circumstances, I am sure that Brian Jack would have paid for towing services and repairs and antifreeze. There is no evidence before the court that he had gone through life trying to clip people who provided him with goods and services.

But on the night of December 17, 1988, there was only one thing on his mind: the disposal of the body.

And, so, after Hudrick and St. Marie had completed the temporary repairs to the Blazer and, on the apparent pretext of test-driving it, the accused left Hudrick's garage and did not return.

In the circumstances that Brian Jack found himself, you may not find it surprising that he neglected to pay his benefactors before taking off into the night.

In his inimitable style, the accomodating young St. Marie, you won't soon forget, recounted the circumstances under which he and Hudrick were ultimately paid.

"So, me and Jimmy waited about ten or 15 minutes," he told you. He smiled engagingly at the jury, obviously enjoying his moment in the spotlight.

"I said to Jimmy, 'This guy is not coming back. He ripped us off.' So, me and Jimmy hopped in the tow truck and we were looking for this guy. But he had told us that he was going to Kenora. See, if he wouldn't have told us that, we'd have no idea where to find this guy. So, we said, 'Ah, he's went [sic] to Kenora.' So, we drove down Highway 1 and we caught him right by the Lilac Motel, about ten minutes away from Jimmy's place."

Paul told you that Jimmy was speeding to catch him and that they saw the Blazer—not going very fast, maybe 80 kilometers per hour; that there was smoke coming from the exhaust pipe.

He said, "It was smoking, like what usually happens when there is antifreeze burning inside the motor."

"So, you catch up to him and what do you do then?" my colleague Kaplan asks, obviously relishing the mood of the moment.

"What we do is we're going to follow him, wait for him to blow it up."

"To blow up the vehicle?"

"Right," said Paul, "and then we were really going to tow him."

Paul St. Marie testified that the person whom he identified as the accused pulled over as soon as the tow truck was driven up behind the Blazer. The accused got out, handed Hudrick a fifty-dollar bill and said, "Will that cover it?"

Paul told you that Jim looked at the stranger, took the money and said, "Yeah."

You will remember him telling you that the accused then got back into his vehicle and proceeded in the direction of the Lilac Motel.

"The last time we saw this Blazer, it was heading east on Number 1 highway. Jim and me got back to Ste. Anne around twelve o'clock or just after twelve," he said.

That Paul St. Marie lacked the polish and sophistication of Harry Williams or Loren Schinkel is self-evident. But as to his powers of observation, attention to detail and capacity to hold an audience, he could bat in their league any day.

Paul St. Marie testified that while he was at Jim Hudrick's place, Roger Pilloud called for the tow truck just after 11:00 p.m.

He and Jim got home around midnight.

These times are particularly significant, ladies and gentlemen, especially in light of the testimony of Mr. Alex Simard, which I will deal with now.

Mr. Simard testified, you will remember, that he entered upon the Trans-Canada Highway, near Hadashville, on Sunday morning, December 18, 1988, between 1:00 and 1:30. He was travelling in a westerly direction. There was hardly any traffic, he said.

While near Hadashville, he caught up to a vehicle which he described as a yellow Jeep, travelling west, and he drove behind it for a while. The driver appeared to him to be very nervous and kept fluctuating his speed. Mr. Simard was of the opinion that the driver of the Jeep wanted to get rid of him.

At one point, this witness said, he passed the yellow vehicle. Later he made a short stop for a tire check and the yellow Jeep passed him. When he caught up to this vehicle a second time, the driver responded in the same fashion, Mr. Simard said.

He noticed what he described as a piece of cloth or towel or blanket

Appendix

over the back bumper on the driver's side, dragging from underneath the tailgate. He said that it was a kind of greenish yellow.

Alex Simard passed the yellow vehicle a second time but eventually stopped for a rest. Once again it went by him.

He was able to view the driver, whom he described as "a real tall man," about 30 to 40 years old.

Now, having rested for approximately ten minutes on the shoulder of the road, Mr. Simard testified that he continued on his journey and within a few miles, he sighted the vehicle again, now approximately 50 to 60 feet off the Trans-Canada Highway and to his right, facing north into the bush.

At this point the witness estimated that he was 45 minutes to one hour from his home. He told you that he lives 13 miles east of Ste. Anne. He also told you that he arrived home at 2:30 a.m. sharp.

You may recall Mr. Simard having said that he was not sure if it was cloth or canvas, but he was certain that he saw something on the top of the vehicle when it was 50 feet off to the side and to his right.

Shortly thereafter, Mr. Simard revealed, he was watching television with his wife. Suddenly, a picture of the Jack vehicle flashed onto the screen.

"That's the truck I followed on December 18," he exclaimed.

Counsel showed him photographs 48 and 59 and asked him if the vehicle in the photos was similar to the vehicle he followed.

You will recall Mr. Simard's answer: "It's exactly the same!"

Ladies and gentlemen, I know that you will give serious consideration to the various time frames because they are vitally important: Roger Pilloud's telephone call to Jim Hudrick shortly after 11:00 p.m. on Saturday night, December 17; the mechanics' arrival back in Ste. Anne around twelve o'clock as the accused drove the smoking Blazer beyond Hadashville; and then Alex Simard observing the yellow vehicle travelling westbound on the Trans-Canada Highway between 1:00 and 1:30 and his arrival at his home at 2:30 sharp.

The significance of these time estimates becomes all the more apparent in light of the testimony of David Lloyd Knechtel, a former Winnipeg Blue Bomber and friend of Brian Jack.

The thoughtful Mr. Knechtel took the accused to the Red Top Drive-In for lunch on Friday, December 23, to offer him a little moral support.

"Brian said that Chris left the house around 9:30, that he had fallen asleep and had awakened around 3:00 or 3:30, and that she had not returned," the sympathetic David Knechtel informed you.

The crafty Brian Jack never missed an opportunity to lie about his whereabouts on that fateful Saturday night and Sunday morning. He continuously lied in his futile endeavour to cover his tracks.

This time he lied to his old football buddy.

Well, ladies and gentlemen, by Friday, December 23, 1988, the fact of Christine Jack's disappearance and the vanishing of the Blazer as well had become the subject of much publicity. And then, the evidence revealed, a man giving the name "Henry" reported to the police that the vehicle in question was on the Salisbury House lot at St. Anne's Road and Fermor Avenue. This indeed, as you well know, turned out to be the case.

Subsequent investigation resulted in the police reaching the conclusion that the caller who used the fictitious name Henry was, in fact, the accused, Brian Jack.

I know that you will study exhibit 112, the tape recording of the anonymous call.

You will be able to again listen to the cassette tapes, which you will have with you during your deliberations.

I would ask you to listen very carefully to Exhibit 113, the recording of the call concerning the location of the Blazer, and Exhibit 114, the recording of the conversation between the accused and Sergeant Mike Hatcher on December 23.

Exhibit 115 is a transcript of the two tape recordings which you will be able to read and study.

And while you are doing that, I would like you to give your attention particularly to a comment that the accused made which you will find at the top of page two of Exhibit 115.

He and the sergeant were talking about the Blazer having been found at the Salisbury House at St. Anne's and Fermor.

"It was—you know, I went down—I went by there a couple of times and never..." Jack sighed and his voice trailed off.

"Did you? Did you see it then?" Sergeant Hatcher pressed.

"No, no—well, I didn't—I, I don't know," Jack spluttered. "I—you know, I didn't. I—it didn't dawn on me but I've, I've driven all over the place back in there and I mean, uh, how could it—how could they have missed it for a week?"

Yes, ladies and gentlemen, the Blazer was at the Salisbury House lot since early Sunday morning, December 18, almost a week.

"How could they have missed it for a week?" the accused asked.

How did Brian Jack know that the vehicle had been there for a week?

How did he know the vehicle's location? Very simply. He parked it there early Sunday morning.

Why, you may well ask yourselves, would he have called in the location of the vehicle?

I don't know. It is not for the Crown to speculate. It just deals in proven facts and it is a proven fact that the accused himself announced its location to the police.

Brian Jack is a well-educated man. He holds a Bachelor of Arts degree in Economics and Physical Education. He has taught school in Winnipeg.

Do you actually believe that this learned man customarily interjects "ah" and "um" and sighs into his everyday conversation?

Mr. Wolson appears to have tried to convince you that that is the case.

In his cross-examination of Patricia Gagné, he wanted to know if Brian stops and says "ah, ah" when he talks.

Mr. Wolson asked Annette Clay, "When Brian talks, does he pause and go "ah, ah."

He even put the same question to Brenda Appleyard, who had spoken to the man but once in her life and even then only for a few minutes.

No, Miss Appleyard didn't recall the accused talking with a bunch of pauses and "ah" and "uh" in his conversation.

Why, Mr. Wolson even asked Roger Pilloud about Brian Jack's hesitating and faltering speech.

I don't recall Peter or Donna Henry or David or Cheryl MacMillan or Aunt Lidijia, who all knew Brian so well, ever saying that he laced his sentences constantly with pauses and "um" and "ahs."

No, ladies and gentlemen, Brian Jack only spluttered and faltered and umed and ahed and repeated himself when one of the sergeants, Paulishyn or Hatcher, trapped him in one of his many lies.

Detective Schinkel testified that on Saturday, December 14, he and his partner, Paulishyn, learned from other officers that by using a digital number recorder, they were able to tell that the call at 5:13 p.m., December 23, 1988, reporting the Blazer's location at the Salisbury House lot at St. Anne's Road and Fermor Avenue, emanated from the accused's home.

Now, you will recall that the officers had conveyed Brian Jack to the Public Safety Building that morning to obtain elimination prints from him.

They spoke to him at this time about the 5:13 p.m. call.

I would ask you to recall some of the testimony in this connection.

Sergeant Paulishyn said to him, "Okay, Brian, you know we found your vehicle."

"Yeah, last night," the accused replied. "I talked to Sergeant Hatcher."

Later on in the conversation, Paulishyn said, "Brian, you made the phone call to report where the vehicle was found."

"Huh? What?" Jack responded with mock surprise.

I hope that you will bear with me, ladies and gentlemen of the jury, as I repeat telling portions of the conversation as between a persistent Paulishyn and an evasive suspect:

"Brian, we have the call on tape."
"I thought all your calls were on tape."
"You reported the location of the vehicle."
"No way."
"Brian, the anonymous call came from your telephone."
"I, uh, don't know what you're talking about."
"Look, Brian, we have a digital number recorder on your telephone. We know the call came from your house."
"Ah, uh, I don't know what you're talking about. No way."
"Was anybody else at your house before you went to St. Andrews?"
"No."
"Well, then, you had to have made the phone call reporting the Blazer's location."
"I don't know what you're talking about."
"Look, how much clearer can I put this to you? We can prove that the phone call came from your residence. We have the digital number recorder to prove it."

Brian Jack now knew that the jig was up. Still, he stunned the investigators with his seemingly casual indifference: "So I called it in. So what?"

I know that you will give careful consideration to the accused's initial denial that he had reported the location of the vehicle in question.

And I know that you will reflect upon Brian Jack's stock answer, "I don't know what you're talking about."

And I know that you will mull over his ultimate answer: "So, I called it in. So what?"

It is a proven fact that the accused called the police at 5:13 p.m. on December 23.

It is a proven fact that he used a false name.

It is a proven fact that he knew the exact location of the Blazer.

It is a proven fact that he lied to Sergeant Paulishyn about having made the call.

Finally, the accused admitted that he had, in fact, made the call.

All of these proven facts will be considered by you, I know, along with

Appendix

all of the other proven facts, facts from which it is open to you to draw the logical inference that Brian Jack was very much involved in his wife's disappearance.

You may find his insistence that he stayed at home all night incredible. You may be satisfied that it was he who drove the Blazer away from 170 Alburg Drive on the night of December 17, 1988. You may have become convinced that he is snarled in a web of circumstantial evidence from which he cannot be disentangled.

The discovery of the Blazer led to some additional evidence further implicating the accused, ladies and gentlemen.

When the vehicle was first examined by police, the doors were unlocked and the driver's seat was found to be extended in its rear-most position.

Cheryl MacMillan, when asked to describe Christine Jack, said that she was five feet, eight inches tall. That Brian Jack is substantially taller is self-evident.

The position of the seat is yet another factor for you to consider, bearing in mind the testimony of the Ste. Anne witnesses concerning the height of the driver of the vehicle on the night of December 17, 1988.

An examination of the interior of the vehicle revealed, you will recall, a dark-coloured spot on the driver's side of the tailgate. Samples were taken from the tailgate area and a number of these samples, as well as samples taken from the lip moulding at the rear of the cargo area, tested out as human blood. On Exhibit 22, the rug or blanket, a thin smear, approximately one and a half by two centimeters, was identified as human blood.

In order to test these samples beyond merely ascertaining whether they were samples of blood and human in origin, it was necessary to obtain a standard.

It will come back to you, I am sure, that during the search of the Jack residence, officers found, in the laundry room in a Tide box used as a garbage receptacle, a sanitary napkin wrapped in a Kleenex. The Tide box can be seen in Exhibit 1A, photograph 30, the box behind and to the immediate right of the laundry hamper.

Mr. Phillip Hodge, the scientist from the R.C.M.P. Crime Detection Laboratory and expert in serology, the scientific study of blood and body fluids, their typing and analysis, used the blood in the sanitary napkin as a standard.

By using this standard, Mr. Hodge testified that he identified a particularly rare blood typing factor in the Erythroocyte Acid Phosphatase (E.A.P.) blood typing system. With this factor alone, he told you, the frequency distribution of the population that would have this factor would be three percent.

In order to attempt to provide a standard from which to carry out further sampling, blood samples, as you heard, were taken from each of the Jack children, Adam and Kairsten.

Based on further testing by the likable scientist, we learned that the Jack children have a biological relationship with the source of the standard used in this case.

The evidence of a biological connection, combined with the fact that there was only one female adult who had been living in the Jack residence prior to Christine Jack's disappearance, namely Christine herself, lends itself to further inferences which you may wish to draw.

Of course, Mr. Wolson will no doubt caution you to be very skeptical of this standard, the sanitary napkin. You will recall that he cross-examined Mrs. MacMillan on this very subject. He alluded to women attending Kinderspirit parties and he even questioned her about adult guests who might have stayed with the children.

My Lord, the Chief Justice, you will recall, asked Mrs. MacMillan if she happened to know her own blood type.

"O," she replied.

Mr. Hodge went one step beyond, however, and told you of a further biological relationship.

He stated that he had obtained liquid blood samples from Christine's parents, Stephan and Veletei Reiter.

He told you that these samples are consistent with being from the parents of the source of blood found on the tailgate of the Blazer, the pillow stuffing (Exhibit 55B) and the standard, the sanitary napkin, which the Crown contends belonged to Christine Jack and no one else.

This is not a mere coincidence, ladies and gentlemen. It is not a coincidence at all.

In light of the serological evidence presented in this case, you may conclude that when Mr. Wolson questions the reliability of this standard, he is indulging in some rather wild speculation.

Blood consistent with having come from the source of the standard is found in two unique places—the tailgate of the Chevy Blazer and the pillow stuffing.

I referred earlier to Constable Paquette's evidence. He testified that on December 22, the accused related how, because he was upset over his wife having left on December 17, he spilled coffee on the couch in the family room. And you will remember that he also told David MacMillan about the spilled coffee.

During the course of their investigations, the police found in the family room a pillow cover which was separated from the pillow itself and was atop a small brownish table. These items can be seen in photographs 37 and 38.

As well, they found cushions and their covers sitting on the seat portion of the hideaway sofa bed in the family room. They are quite visible in photographs 37, 38 and 39.

The covering for the couch cushion was turned inside out. Constable Luczenczyn testified that the cover appeared to have been washed and smelled of Downy or some other anti-static substance.

A closer examination of the pillow found on the brown table uncovered a depression in the centre of the cushion, a round hole within which a red substance was found.

I go back to Constable Luczenczyn's evidence. According to him, it appeared as if someone had pulled a piece out. There were fibres all around. The area pulled out was approximately one inch in diameter and two inches deep. The outer portion of the pillow had a faint mark that corresponded in position with the location in the pillow from which the filling was pulled out. Indeed, when the cover was placed over the top of the batting, they corresponded.

The pillow stuffing was submitted for laboratory examination. Human blood was located in the pillow stuffing and it was determined that it could not have originated from the Jack children, Adam or Kairsten.

However, Mr. Hodge told you that the typing factors identified from the children's blood were consistent with their sources having a biological relationship with whoever produced the blood on the sanitary napkin and the pillow stuffing. He defined the term "biological relationship," as meaning a mother or father relationship and/or a son or daughter relationship.

The expert in serology defined the term "consistent with" for his purposes as meaning that the finding does not carry with it the confidence of a conclusion, as for example in the science of fingerprints. Nevertheless, in the context of the various pieces of evidence which he examined and tested, the findings are very significant.

At the end of the day, of course, it will be for you, the members of the jury, to attach the weight to Mr. Hodge's evidence which you feel it warrants.

Now, the laboratory examination of the pillow cover which seemed to align with the pillow showed up a relatively large area of what was described as thin staining. However, nothing more conclusive than a positive presumptive test result for blood could be obtained, that is, on the cover. Mr. Hodge testified that he had done an understudy test of machine washing of blood stains and found that it usually removed all typing factors.

In this connection, I would remind you again of Constable Luczenczyn's observation that all the pillows appeared to have been washed.

In view of the findings on the pillow stuffing, the fact that blood was found on a vase located under the table, on which the pillow was lying, is of some significance, I suggest, even though the evidence is silent as to whether or not it is human blood.

A similar result was achieved on a sample of stain removed from the arm rest and back portion of the family room couch.

The man from the crime lab was able to assign an outside limit to the time when the blood stained the pillow. He carried out his examination in April 1989 and, in his opinion, the stain originated within six months of that date.

You can see the blood on the vase in photographs 38 and 43.

There is blood on the vase, blood on the pillow cover, blood on the pillow stuffing. More pieces fitting securely into this jigsaw puzzle, this case of circumstantial evidence.

And from the cumulative effect of all of these pieces of circumstantial evidence, I respectfully submit that you can draw the logical inference that the homicide was committed within the family room of the Jack residence.

❖ ❖ ❖ ❖ ❖

Earl Joseph Weber is a citizen of the United States of America, currently residing in Grand Forks, North Dakota.

He voluntarily and, in fact, obligingly arranged to come to Winnipeg to testify in this trial.

He told you that he and Christine Reiter were both students at the University of North Dakota back in 1973. They became engaged to each other on no less than two occasions.

However, as you learned, they subsequently went their separate ways.

Nevertheless, obviously they hadn't forgotten each other. A spark still remained despite the passing years.

I don't propose to review his testimony. You will remember it.

But let me say this: There was one reason and only one reason why the Crown wanted you to see and hear from Mr. Weber.

It was important that he tell you himself that he had not seen Christine

Jack since Sunday morning, November 20, 1988, when they sat in his truck and chatted for an hour and a half outside her hotel.

And it was important that he tell you that apart from telephone conversations he had with her in early December of 1988, subsequent to her return to Winnipeg, he had not heard from her.

Incidentally, ladies and gentlemen, you will remember that my friend Richard Wolson showed Brenda Appleyard a picture of Earl Weber. Was he perhaps indulging in a little more wild speculation or was he, to borrow one of his own expressions, off on another wild goose chase?

No, Earl Weber has been unable to communicate with Christine Jack since December 17, 1988, like everybody else.

My friend will stress over and over again when he addresses you, I am certain, that the Crown is asking you to embark upon a course of speculation and guesswork, and that there is no room for guesswork or speculation in a court of law.

Of course there is no room for conjecture in a court of law.

But inevitably my learned friend himself will invite you to indulge in some rather fanciful speculation.

No doubt he will refer to some of the questions he put to Cheryl MacMillan on cross-examination and to some of her answers.

Cheryl said, as you know, that Chris was five feet, eight inches tall and long-legged. She didn't ever recall Chris having moved the seat in the Blazer.

Does my friend expect that you will glean from this that the seat was never in any other than the far-back position?

Cheryl found it unusual, she told Mr. Wolson, that Chris had not called home while she was away in Grand Forks on the November eighteenth weekend.

You may not find it at all unusual, however, having regard to your knowledge of the strain she was under at the time.

Are you to glean from Mr. Wolson's question and the answer he received that Christine wasn't really all that concerned about her youngsters despite what everyone else told you about this loving mother?

Oh, yes, and my learned friend elicited from Cheryl MacMillan that Chris was open, carefree, wasn't nervous and pretty trusting of strangers. I believe her exact words were, "In terms of talking to strangers, Chris was not being as cautious as she should have been."

Would Mr. Wolson have you speculate from this comment that there was the possibility that Christine Jack's last encounter was with a total stranger?

Well, it wasn't, ladies and gentlemen, and there is overwhelming evidence to prove it.

Her last encounter, the fatal encounter, was with the accused himself, her husband, Brian Jack.

❖ ❖ ❖ ❖ ❖

I would now like to say something to you about the testimony of the psychiatrist, Dr. James McPhee, and the lawyer, Mrs. Janice Dewar.

Dr. McPhee saw Christine Jack on Tuesday, December 13, just four days before she was murdered.

Mrs. Dewar saw her on Wednesday, December 14, just three days before her murder.

Christine's next appointment with Dr. McPhee was scheduled for Tuesday, December 20, an appointment that her death kept her from keeping.

Mrs. Dewar stated that she called Christine on Friday, December 16, and left a message. Later that afternoon Christine returned her call and left a message in which she indicated that she would phone again the following Monday, December 19, a call that her death kept her from making.

There are so many, many things for you to consider in your deliberations, so many, many pieces to be fitted together in this puzzle.

Among those things there are certain observations that both Dr. McPhee and Mrs. Dewar made about Christine that I know you will consider.

First, with respect to Dr. McPhee's testimony, and you will recall that he carries on a private practice of psychiatry, teaches in the Faculty of Medicine at the University of Manitoba, works at the Child Guidance Clinic and does marriage counselling. And he saw Christine and Brian Jack in his role as a marriage counsellor. Nevertheless, as a qualified psychiatrist, he commented on Christine Jack's emotional state, just as the trained psychologist Alfred Kircher did.

Dr. McPhee saw in Christine Jack, as did Mr. Kircher, no sign of any psychosis. Maybe some stress but she was functioning very well. He detected no sign of mental illness, no evidence of biological stress, no need for hospitalization or medication, no sign of clinical depression.

He said that she was emotionally responding to her stress, that she was not suicidal. Added to her wellness, she was optimistic about her future and she absolutely intended to go on living.

Janice Dewar specializes in family law, that branch of the law which deals with divorce and separation.

On Wednesday, December 14, Mrs. Dewar spent almost an hour and a half with Christine, advising her as to her various options and explaining the law with respect to divorce, custody of children, maintenance, division of property and the possibility of a restraining order.

Mrs. Dewar observed that her client was clearly under some stress, as are most people in similar circumstances.

She found Christine to have been very intelligent, understanding of the options open to her and calm.

Mrs. Dewar said, and I quote her exact words:

Clearly, she had made up her mind where she was going and what she was going to do and that came through clearly. Her mind was made up. There was no doubt in my mind that she would call me again.

No, ladies and gentlemen, Christine Jack was not clinically depressed on Saturday, December 17, 1988.

That she was emotionally drained and under a lot of stress because of a flawed marriage, there can be no doubt.

But she was not suicidal.

She was not clinically depressed.

She had not planned to abandon her children and run off with some other man.

She loved her children. She was planning for their future continuously.

And she had the stamina to carry on.

I have already spoken of her last letter to her mother and father, which she wrote on December 16 but never mailed: "I'm finding out that I have more strength and determination than I realized."

Death robbed her of her strength!

Her murderer shattered her dreams of a better life for her children and her.

❖ ❖ ❖ ❖ ❖

Ladies and gentlemen of the jury:

My colleague, Mr. Brian Kaplan, and I wish more than anything else that we were not here today asking you to find as a fact that Christine Anna Jack is dead.

We wish, as each and every one of you do, that she were alive, that she could be with young Adam and Kairsten, watching over them as they continue to grow.

So do all of the people whose lives were enriched by her presence.

It is not to be.

Christine Anna Jack is dead. She died at the hands of her husband, the accused, just eight days before Christmas on December 17, 1988.

Thank you.

Thank you, My Lord.

Endnotes

1. *Regina v. Commissioner of Police of the Metropolis Ex Parte Blackburn* (no. 2) (1968) 2 Q.B. 150, 155.
2. Goldenson, Robert M. *The Encyclopedia of Human Behavior*. Vol. 1. New York: Doubleday & Co., 1970. 711.
3. Menninger, Karl, *The Vital Balance: The Life Process in Mental Health and Illness*. New York. Viking Press, 1963.
4. Clemens, S.L. "The Private History of a Campaign That Failed," *Collected Tales, Sketches, Speeches and Essays, 1852-1890*. Library of America, 1960.
5. Browning, Michael and Dr. William R. Maples. *Dead Men Do Tell Tales*. New York: Doubleday, 1995.
6. *Regina v. Caccamo* (1975) 1 S.C.R. 786.
7. *Regina v. Stinchcombe* 68 C.C.C. (3d) 1.
8. Doyle, Arthur Conan. "A Case of Identity," in *The Original Illustrated Sherlock Holmes*. Secaucus, NJ: Castle Books, 1978.
9. Weinbert, Arthur. *Attorney for the Damned*. New York: Simon and Schuster, 1957.
10. Shakespeare, William, *Henry VI* - Pt. II, Act IV, Sc. 2.
11. Stephen, James F. *A General View of the Criminal Law of England*. (2nd Ed) London, 1890. 170.
12. *Rex v. Wright*, 33 Cr. App. Rep. 22.
13. *Regina v. Jack*, 70 C.C.C. (3d) 108.
14. *Winnipeg Free Press*, 21 July 1992.
15. *Regina v. Jack*, 70 C.C.C. (3d) 67.
17. *The Holy Bible*, Ecclesiastes 10:12.
18. Dickens, Charles. *Oliver Twist*. London: Penguin Books, 1966.
19. *Winnipeg Sun*, 31 October 1992.
20. 88 *Manitoba Report* (2d) 96.
21. 13 *Manitoba Report* (2d) 88.

Trials & Errors: The People vs. Brian Gordon Jack

[22] Bacon, Francis, "Lord Bacon's Advice to Justice Hutton Marshall Brown," *Wit and Humor of Bench and Bar*, 1899.

[23] 13 *Manitoba Report* (2d) 91.

[24] *Winnipeg Free Press*, 21 July 1992.

[25] Rice, Grantland. "Alumnus Football," in *Football's Best Short Stories*. ed. Paul D. Stawdohar. Chicago: Chicago Review Press, 1998, 1-3.

[26] Osborn, Albert S. *Mind of a Juror.* Littleton, CO: Fred B. Rothman & Co. Publishing, 1982.

[27] Lincoln, Abraham. (speech given at Clinton, IL, 2 September 1858).

Index

A

Abbott, Supreme Court Justice, 128
Adams, John Quincy, 62
Adventures of Pinocchio, The, 38
Anonymous phone call, 33–34, 37–38, 41, 178, 180–181
Appeal
  of bail decision, 101
  of first trial, 96
  of second trial, 116
  of third trial, 124, 125–129, 130–132
Appleyard, Brenda, 21–22, 51, 66, 154, 163–164, 167, 170, 174, 175, 179, 185

B

Bacon, Francis, 123
Baden, Dr. Michael, 54
Barker, Eddie, 36
Bergman, Assistant Commissioner R.A., 110
Blazer (*see* Chevy Blazer), 133
Blood typing evidence, 181–184
Butler, Samuel, 16

C

Camrie, James, 170
Charter House witnesses (*see also* Garbutt, Pike, Gershman), 101–104
Charter of Rights and Freedoms, 131, 133
Chesterfield, Lord, 55, 61
Chevy Blazer, 20–23, 25, 27, 30, 31, 33–36, 40–42, 43, 47–50, 89, 101–102, 103, 122–123, 140, 147, 148, 152, 153–154, 163, 169, 170–181, 182, 185
Clay, Annette, 14, 78, 80, 81, 145, 146, 150, 151, 160, 162, 179
Closing address
  crown counsel, 73–74, 139–188
  defence, 75–92
Collerman, Judge Howard, 78, 79
Confucius, 29
Corneille, Pierre, 27
Court of Appeal, 118, 125, 134
  Philp decision, 97
Cowlings, Al, 72
Creighton, Cst. Lawrence, 48–49, 51, 52, 164, 169, 171, 172, 174
Cyncora, Det. Brian, 31

D

Dangerfield, J.G.B. (George), 55, 113, 120, 138
Darichuk, Mr. Justice Wallace M., 9, 114, 118
  misdirection of jury, 10, 116–117
Darrow, Clarence, 75, 91–92
Denning, Lord, 11
Dewar, Janice, 186–187
Dickens, Charles, 108
DNA evidence, 108–110, 114, 116

E

Ecclesiastes 10:13, 106
Ecclesiasticus XXXII: 8, 73
Encyclopedia of Human Behavior, The, 38
Ewatski, Staff Sgt. Jack, 45–46

Trials & Errors: The People vs. Brian Gordon Jack

F

Fauteux, Supreme Court Justice, 128
Fenelon, Franÿois, 73
Fingerprint evidence, 108–109
Forensic evidence, 36, 44, 155, 181–184
Foster, Garry, 53
Frizzell, Cst. George, 27–28, 29

G

Gagné, Patricia, 78, 179
Garbutt, Shirley, 68–70, 72, 88, 91, 100, 102, 120, 166
Gershman, George, 72
Goddard, Lord Chief justice, 94
Goldenson, Robert M., 38
Greenlay, Wayne, 171
Gregoire, Gilbert, 21, 167
Gresson, Cst. Donald, 29, 148, 151

H

Hall, Supreme Court Justice, 128
Harden, Bud, 27
Harden, Fay, 14, 19, 27, 145, 146
Hatcher, Sgt. Mike, 34–35, 41, 78, 178, 179
Hebert, Cst., 49, 51
Helper, Madam Justice Bonnie, 126, 127, 128, 133
Henry (anonymous caller), 34, 35, 178
Henry, Assistant Commissioner J.B.D., 110
Henry, Donna Mae, 14, 19, 24, 26–27, 38, 58–59, 61, 80, 82, 87, 135, 145, 146, 151, 152, 155, 156, 157, 160–161, 179
Henry, Lauren, 146, 157
Henry, Peter, 19, 24, 26, 80, 85, 87, 135, 150, 151, 153, 161–162, 174, 179
Hewak, Chief Justice Benjamin, 9, 56, 68, 69, 70, 74, 99–100
 charge to the jury, 93–95
Hodge, Phil, 109–110, 181, 183–184
Hogland, Cst. Ronald, 29, 148, 151
Holmes, Justice Oliver Wendell, 98
Holmes, Sherlock, 68
Hubard, Mr. Justice Charles, 126, 127
Hudrick, Jim, 21–23, 47–50, 52, 102, 165, 169–170, 171–173, 174, 175–176

I

Ingersoll, Robert, 133

J

Jack, Adam, 14, 15, 18, 30, 45, 46, 61, 65, 71, 75, 76, 80, 87, 108, 111, 115, 135, 138, 143, 144, 145, 182, 183, 187
Jack, Brian Gordon, 9, 12, 15, 26, 34–35, 36, 44, 45–46, 47, 52, 62, 75, 76, 79, 90, 106, 115, 125, 134, 137, 139, 142, 147, 154, 164, 178, 179, 186
 arrest, 51
 first trial, 55–95
 history of marriage, 160, 161–162
 identification, 47, 49, 51, 66, 102, 154, 165–170
 initial statement, 16–19
 interrogation, 37–38, 39–40, 40–41, 42, 180
 letter to Christine's father, 158–159
 missing person claim, 27–28, 29–32, 148
 night of Christine's disappearance, 18–19, 20–23, 20–23, 25–26, 85, 140–141, 148, 155
 profile, 77–78
 Supreme Court ruling, 11, 133
Jack, Christine Anna, 9, 13, 26, 30, 31, 40, 41, 43, 51, 54, 58–59, 62, 65, 75, 76, 82, 84, 90, 106, 107, 115, 135, 138, 142, 156, 157, 181, 182, 184, 186–187
 background, 145–146
 cause of death, 25
 disposal of body, 12, 52, 56, 62, 143, 163
 history of marriage, 17–18, 59–60, 61, 140, 144, 161
 letter to parents, 14–15, 158
 night of her disappearance, 18–20, 24, 26, 60, 121, 140–142
 reported missing, 27
 sighting at Charter House, 68–72, 83, 91, 102, 105, 110, 122, 166
Jack, Kairsten, 14, 15, 30, 45, 46, 61, 65, 71, 75, 76, 80, 87, 111, 115, 135,

Index

138, 143, 144, 145, 157, 182, 183, 187
Jackal, The, 29
Jankovec, Lidijia, 14, 19, 26, 59–61, 80, 112, 135, 144, 145–146, 151, 153, 155, 161, 162, 179
Jefferson, Thomas, 75, 100, 133
Johnson, Dr. Samuel, 14
Johnson, Sgt. Paul, 31
Judson, Supreme Court Justice, 128
Jury deadlock, 121

K

Kaplan, Brian "Beanie", 14, 57, 62, 63, 66–67, 68, 69–70, 71, 79, 91, 110–112, 120–121, 138, 145, 149, 152, 162, 164, 168, 171, 176, 187
Kashuba, Cst. Darlene, 25, 29–30, 147, 148–149, 150, 151
Keats, John, 13
Kircher, Alfred, 83, 156
Knechtel, David Lloyd, 80, 87, 151, 177

L

Lamer, Chief Justice Antonio, 11, 12, 98, 133, 135, 138
Lapsus Linguae, 117
Laskin, Supreme Court Justice, 128
Les, Dr., 137–138
Levinter, Isadore, 40, 71
L'Heureux-Dubé, Madam Justice, 130, 132
Lincoln, Abraham, 150
Lorenzini, Carlo, 38
Luczenczyn, Cst. Peter, 44–45, 183, 184
Luther, Martin, 126

M

MacMillan, Cheryl, 14, 17, 18, 19, 24, 26, 30–31, 34–36, 39, 58, 61, 65, 80, 81, 84, 86, 92, 135, 145, 146, 151, 154, 157, 179, 181, 182, 185
MacMillan, David, 26, 86, 135, 147, 150, 151, 152, 154, 174, 179
Mansfield, Lord, 101
Maples, Dr. William R., 52, 54
Marshall, Sgt. "Gentleman Bob", 35, 44, 47, 48, 51
Marta (former neighbour), 15

Martland, Supreme Court Justice, 128
McAmmond, John, 113
McInnes, Mr. Justice, 139, 174
McPhee, Dr. James, 18, 156, 158, 186
McTavish, Gordie, 55
Menninger, Karl, 38
Mind of a Juror, The, 141
Molière, 33
Moore, Clement Clarke, 43
Morrison, Robert Clinton, 120, 121, 138
Muller, Max, 24
Munroe, Cst., 163

N

Napoleon, 74
News reports, 43, 65–66, 98–99, 114–115, 126–127

O

Ogston, James, 80
O'Sullivan, Mr. Justice Joseph, 98, 110–111
 appeal judgment, 106–108

P

Paquette, Cst. Jay, 25, 30–31, 139–140, 144, 147, 149–150, 151, 155
Paulishyn, Sgt. Edward, 16, 27, 31–32, 34, 35, 39–42, 44, 52, 78, 81, 82, 89, 179
Pelland, Cst. James, 29–30, 147, 148–149, 151
Philp, Mr. Justice Allan, 96, 98, 107
Piché, Armand, 57
Pigeon, Supreme Court Justice, 128
Pike, Donna, 68, 69, 70–71, 72, 88, 91–92, 100, 102, 166
Pilloud, Roger, 21–22, 51, 66, 154, 163, 164–165, 167, 169, 170, 174, 175, 176, 179

R

Rabbit, The, 55, 130
Regina v. Caccamo, 63
Reiter, Stephan, 14, 59, 61, 80, 135, 143, 146, 158–159, 182
Reiter, Veletei, 14, 30, 59, 60, 61, 112, 135, 143, 146, 151, 182
Rice, Grantland, 137

Trials & Errors: The People vs. Brian Gordon Jack

Ritchie, Supreme Court Justice, 128

S

Saull, Richard, 104, 113, 138
Schindel, Reid, 80, 84, 146, 151
Schinkel, Det. Loren, 16, 31, 34, 35–36, 39, 40, 44, 47–48, 52, 78, 81, 82, 89, 105, 138, 176
Scollin, Mr. Justice John Ambrose, 10, 120, 121, 124, 128–129, 134
  charge to jury, 121–123
Scott, Chief Justice Richard, 93, 97, 98, 100, 108
  appeal judgment, first, 101–102, 104, 107, 109, 117, 118
  appeal judgment, third, 125–126, 127–128, 131–132
Search for the body, 52–54
Second trial, 113–119
Sentence
  first trial, 96
  third trial, 124, 132
Shakespeare, William, 20
Simard, Alex, 176–177
Simard, Murielle, 21, 154, 165–166, 170
Simard, Patrick Joseph, 21–22, 154, 165–166, 167–168, 170, 174
Simpson, O.J., 72
Sopinka, Mr. Justice John, 66–67
Speirs, Sgt. "Big John", 35, 44–46, 47, 48, 51, 54
Spence, Supreme Court Justice, 128
Spencer, Herbert, 120
Sporer, Nancy, 16–17
St. Marie, Paul, 22, 47–50, 51, 52, 102, 154, 169, 171, 172–173, 175–176
Ste. Anne witnesses (*see also* Hudrick, St. Marie, Pilloud, Appleyard), 101–104
Stellman, Dan, 53
Stephen, Sir James F., 94, 95
Supreme Court of Canada, 10, 11, 63, 119, 121, 128, 131, 133–135

T

Taylor, "Reverend" Jack, 39
Third trial, 116, 120–124
Thompson, Robert, 44–45
Thoreau, Henry David, 47

Twain, Mark, 41

V

Vandergraaf, "Reverend" Peter, 39
Verdict
  first trial, 96
  second trial, 115, 117, 125
  third trial, 124

W

Walz, Katherine, 80, 147, 151, 159–160
Weber, Earl Joseph, 58, 62–67, 68, 84, 106, 107, 121, 144, 184–185
Williams, Sgt. Harry, 48, 49–50, 51, 52–53, 164–169, 170, 171, 172, 176
Wolson, Richard "Tiger", 56–57, 60, 63, 64, 66, 68, 75–83, 84, 94, 96, 105, 109, 113, 115–116, 119, 121, 123, 142, 144, 153, 155, 156, 165, 166, 168, 170, 173, 174, 179, 182, 185

John D. (Jack) Montgomery, Q.C. is a former Chief Prosecutor for the City of Winnipeg; Provincial Director of Criminal Prosecutions; and a General Counsel in Manitoba's Department of Justice. His previous book, *She Was Only Three: The Trials of John Thomas James Jr.*, was published in 1998.